The
Joy
Principle

Ken Wilson, Ph.D.

The Joy Principle

Lessons from the
Book of Philippians

Published by

AGAPE PUBLISHING
PO Box 1433
Puyallup, Washington 98371

Copyright © 2011 Ken Wilson, Ph.D.

All rights reserved. No portion of this book may be reproduced in any form without the written permission of the publisher, including translation.

All Scripture quotations, unless otherwise noted, are taken from the New International Version © 1986 by Holman Bible Publishers, all rights reserved.

All rights reserved.
First Edition 2011

ISBN: 978-0-925449-22-1 (pbk.)

Cover design and text formatting by
    Beth E. Miller, iGs Graphic Designs

Acknowledgments

I first want to dedicate this book to my lovely wife Sandy, who has supported me in my ministry for over 40 years. I am indebted to her for her strength in the faith and her wise counsel to me on my books and other aspects of my ministry. I also want to dedicate this book to my wonderful children: Anthony, Troy, Eric, and Tawnya, and my grandchildren of whom I am very proud. They have been my pride and joy and I thank God for them.

Many of the thoughts and ideas in this book have been collected over an extended period of time. Some of this information comes from other sources originally, but I don't remember what they are or who they were. I am indebted to them, whomever and whatever, because they have contributed to my learning and this book.

I also want to acknowledge my friend and scholar Wayne Jackson, whom I quote frequently, and who has been an inspiration to me with his writings and especially with his wonderfully written and scholarly presented commentary on the book of Philippians. It is entitled, *Rejoice With Me*, and is probably the best commentary I have read on this book.

Acknowledgements would not be complete without mentioning Paris Rogers, our Office Manager and Stephanie Fahnstrom, our Distance Learning Coordinator in the office of Agape Publishing Company. They have both been very helpful in processing and developing this book. I am so thankful for both of them and our staff at Agape Counseling Center.

I present this book as a work of JOY in the preparation and research of my favorite New Testament epistle. I have used the book of Philippians as the main biblical resource in my counseling and teaching ministry. This book is the apostle Paul's most intimate revelation about his ministry and the most educational of his writings in reference to dealing with life and circumstances that we all face every day.

Paul's comprehensive description of the mind of Christ presents a powerful example of being a humble servant of God. The book of Philippians is one of Paul's greatest achievements in his writing efforts, because it best defines the mindset and the power of choosing to be JOYFUL in spite of circumstances. Therefore, I must emphasize the privilege of acknowledging Paul's inspired achievement with the book of Philippians, for it has helped strengthen me in my service to Christ and empowered my counseling ministry.

Introduction

Philippians is a book filled with joy and encouragement in the midst of trial and tribulation. Paul expresses his love for the Philippian church and appreciates their support and stand in the Christian faith. The external and internal evidence for the fact that Paul is the author of this epistle is basically unchallenged. There is very little doubt in the minds of recognized scholars that this is a fact.

In 356 B.C., King Philip of Macedonia (the father of Alexander the Great) took this town and expanded it, renaming it Philippi. The Romans captured it in 168 B.C., and in 42 B.C., the defeat of the forces of Brutus and Cassius by those of Anthony and Octavian (later named Augustus) took place outside the city. Augustus turned Philippi into a Roman colony, and a military outpost. The citizens of this colony were regarded as citizens of Rome and given a number of special privileges. Philippi was a military city and a commercial center. Evidently there were not enough Jews to meet the requirements for starting a synagogue when Paul arrived there (Acts 16:13).

The Book of Philippians was written during Paul's imprisonment in Rome. In addition to traditional evidence pointing to the imprisonment in Rome when Philippians was written, there is the internal evidence. Paul states, *"As a result, it has become clear throughout the whole palace guard and to everyone else that I am in chains for Christ"* (Philippians 1:13). And then, *"All the saints send you greetings, especially those who belong to Caesar's household"* (Philippians 4:22).

The key expression in 1:13 is the term "palace (praetorian) guard." They were the emperor's personal body guards, similar to the Secret Service of the President of the United States. The palace guard would guard special prisoners as well as protect the emperor. They were an elite company of soldiers and they represented the emperor as they protected him. It is evident that Paul must have shared the gospel with some of the guard and that through them some of Caesar's household had been converted to Christianity.

Therefore, this epistle seems to have been written during Paul's two-year imprisonment and was probably penned between 62 and 63 A.D. This letter to the Philippians was the most intimate and affectionate of all of Paul's letters. It is a letter that is filled with joy and enthusiasm, with Paul realizing that his imprisonment reveals the wisdom of God and he was experiencing a level of contentment perhaps beyond anything he had experienced before (Philippians 4:11).

There is an inference in Paul's letter to the Philippians that implies a growth pattern to his ministry that reflects a deeper understanding of joy and contentment (Philippians 4:4). In other words, he is transforming in his understanding of contentment and growth in the likeness of Christ (2 Corinthians 3:18). It would seem that Paul is contrasting his experience in prison with the teaching of the world. Paul is learning a facet of contentment that is *God-sufficient*, rather than society's teaching that says contentment comes to a person who learns to be *self-sufficient*. The world believes that contentment is developed by the circumstances in which a person finds himself. Such a belief system is based on the success a man can achieve in the process of *happiness seeking*.

There is a distinction to be made between the terms *joy* and *happiness*. The word *joy* in the New Testament is translated from the Greek word *chara*, and is translated to mean, "joy," or "delight," and is at times by context connected with falling into trials; James 1:2.¹ It is evident that this word *joy* is used as an expression prompted by a relationship with Christ, and not by an experience dependent on circumstances. It is the world's belief that *happiness* is dependent on circumstances.

I titled this book *The Joy Principle*, not only because of the importance of the word JOY in the book of Philippians, but also because of the meaning of the word *principle*. Webster's Dictionary says of *principle*,

> The ultimate source, origin, or cause of something; a natural or original tendency, faculty, or endowment; a fundamental truth, law, doctrine, or motivating force, upon which others are based.²

In other words, the concept of JOY in the life of a Christian is seen in the New Testament as a fundamental truth. It can almost be classified as a doctrinal imperative for the Christian disciple to live by if he/she seeks to be a light of the world (Matthew 5:13-16).

Neil Anderson, editor of the Gospel Advocate states,

> In *Almost Christian*, author Kenda Creasy, Dean of Princeton Theological Seminary, says the beliefs and practices of teens, trouble many church scholars. Her research indicated a majority of teens believe in God but reject Christian doctrines largely because they believe God exists to make them happy.³

This belief system seems to be affecting much of society.

---

[1] W. E. Vine's, Expository Dictionary of New Testament Words, Mac Donald Publishing, 619
[2] Webster's *New World Dictionary*, Second College Edition, 1974
[3] Neil Anderson, an Editorial entitled, *Almost Christian*, Gospel Advocate, October 2010

This book is not a commentary on the book of Philippians. But it is the goal of this author to use Paul's writings in Philippians as a backdrop to emphasize the point that there is peril in seeking happiness first and foremost in our lives. It is a fact that when *happiness seeking* is our main goal in life it leads us down the pathway of self-destruction. It is also true that in our society many believe there is no such thing as an absolute truth. In fact, many people in our world today believe that they, themselves are the final arbiter of truth. It is only how they feel that has any relevancy to truth. It is common to hear that *truth* to one person may not be *truth* to another. Therefore, there is no absolute truth in the minds of many in our culture today; only the opinions of each as they apply to their own lives.

Because feelings have become the standard in our society as to what truth is, we see a growing tendency to judge everything based on the answer to the question, "does it make me happy?" If it doesn't make me happy, then it is not worth pursuing. If it does make me happy, then I should engage in it regardless of how immoral or unbiblical it may be. We see this kind of philosophy seeping into the church today. It is a self-destructive life style and diminishes our trust in God and our respect for His commandments. It reveals in us as Christians, a willingness to rank *happiness seeking* over *truth seeking*. And it is in conflict with our Christian walk (2 Corinthians 5:7).

I hope that this book will be an encouragement and will help strengthen those who read it and that it might build them up in the faith to face tribulation with the conviction that it will reap dividends that prepare us for anything in this life. It is the purpose of this author to help Christians continue to transform into the likeness of Christ, and to reject the standard of the world that proclaims that happiness seeking, at all costs, is the purpose for living. Such a philosophy is the devil's scheme to destroy us.

What then is *The Joy Principle*? The apostle Paul defines it in terms of the benefits of sacrifice when he says,

> *. . . and we rejoice in the hope of the glory of God. Not only so, but we also rejoice in our sufferings, because we know that suffering produces perseverance; perseverance, character; and character, hope. And hope does not disappoint us, because God has poured out his love into our hearts by the Holy Spirit, whom he has given us* (Romans 5:2-5).

And this,

> *What, then, can we say in response to this? If God is for us, who can be against us? He who did not spare his own Son, but gave him up for us all–how will he not also, along with him, graciously gives us all things?* (Romans 8:31, 32).

To all who may read this book, let us give God the glory as we receive the *joy* to be experienced in *truth seeking*.

The apostle Paul tells us, *"Be joyful always; pray continually; give thanks in all circumstances, for this is God's will for you in Christ Jesus"* (1 Thessalonians 5:16-18).

The Book of Philippians

Table of Contents

Lesson		Page
One	Joyfully Thanking God in Prayer.	1
Two	Joyfully Claiming Holiness in Christ.	17
Three	Joyfully Facing the Unexpected.	33
Four	Joyfully Contending for the Faith.	45
Five	Joyfully Possessing the Mind of Christ.	59
Six	Joyfully Shining as the Stars in Heaven.	73
Seven	Joyfully Serving as Christ's Disciple.	85
Eight	Joyfully Knowing Christ Personally.	97
Nine	Joyfully Pressing Toward the Goal.	109
Ten	Joyfully Transforming into Christ.	123
Eleven	Joyfully Praising the Lord Always.	135
Twelve	Joyfully Learning to Be Content.	147
Thirteen	Joyfully Growing in His Grace.	161

Bibliography.. 173

Lesson One
(Chapter 1:1-6)

Joyfully Thanking God in Prayer

Paul and Timothy, servants of Christ Jesus. To all the saints in Christ Jesus at Philippi, together with the overseers and deacons: Grace and peace to you from God our Father and the Lord Jesus Christ.

I thank my God every time I remember you. In all my prayers for all of you, I always pray with joy because of your partnership in the gospel from the first day until now, being confident of this, that he who began a good work in you will carry it on to completion until the day of Christ Jesus.

The most amazing success story in many years has been a little book by Bruce Wilkinson titled, *The Prayer of Jabez*. It is based on two rather obscure verses in 1 Chronicles. Jabez was more honorable than his brothers. His mother had named him Jabez, saying, *'I gave birth to him in pain.'* Jabez cried out to the God of Israel,

Oh, that you would bless me and enlarge my territory! Let your hand be with me, and keep me from harm so that I will be free from pain. And God granted his request (1 Chronicles 4:9, 10).

Most of the people who have reviewed this little book have focused on two phrases: "bless me" and "enlarge my territory." And they have interpreted these two phrases to mean that Wilkinson is preaching a so-called "prosperity gospel." The prosperity gospel sounds something like this: "If you just give your heart to Jesus, you will prosper in every way." This would seem to be the reason that millions of people have bought this book. They think that just by finding a secret formula in Scripture they are going to have it all. Wilkinson says this is definitely not what he had in mind when he wrote the book.

The joy of being blessed in Christ is not based on how much stuff God will give us if we are faithful to Him. It is not based on the gospel of "health and wealth." There is not a promise in Scripture that God's elect will have a smooth road in life without struggles.

The word JOY in the Greek is *chara*, and it means, "delight, gladness, joy" (James 1:2). Determined by usage, the words have a different connotation. "Happiness" is usually equated with the circumstances one experiences, and "joy" is connected with emotions related to relationships regardless of the circumstances.

This letter opens with greetings to the church at Philippi from Paul and Timothy. Timothy is his young companion in the gospel, a convert of the apostle from the city of Lystra (Acts 16:1; 1 Timothy 1:2). Paul starts off stating that he is a servant of Jesus Christ. Paul and Timothy were servants (slaves, Greek word *doulos*) who belonged to Christ and they would both be surprised that having given their lives to Jesus, they should expect the blessings of prosperity and freedom from pain. Paul himself is a prisoner in chains (1:13).

The Philippian church had its period of persecution in which two preachers where thrown in jail (Acts 16:16-40) and now, ten years later, the Philippians again face agonizing opposition (1:28-30). Yet in the middle of it all, Paul proclaims peace, not through prosperity in the future, but as a present reality in his state of imprisonment. In other words, peace and prosperity are not found in the absence of pain and suffering, but in the blessings of God in Christ Jesus. As Paul reflects upon his earlier associations with the brethren at Philippi, he cannot but thank God for their fellowship with him in the furtherance of the gospel.

Biblical scholar Wayne Jackson, authored an excellent commentary on the book of Philippians, and he states,

> The verb 'thank' is here in the present tense, denoting Paul's abiding gratitude for these beloved saints. The apostle refers to Jehovah as 'my God,' affirming a very personal relationship with his heavenly Father.[4]

There is something about His children being thankful that especially impresses God. Because we must live in this world, we can be very heavily influenced by this ungrateful society's attitudes. Do we really appreciate all that we have been given? Are we sincerely thankful to our great God for the many blessings He has so bountifully poured out upon us?

One of Paul's great qualities was a thankful heart. He implores us as disciples to be continually thankful in all circumstances (1Thessalonians 5:18; Colossians 3:15; 4:2). James also challenges us to be thankful even in trials and tribulations and to be joyful as well (James 1:2-5). The principle of thanking God without ceasing means often and for everything. Anytime is appropriate. Nevertheless, the principle of balance holds true as well. Thanksgiving would

---

[4] Wayne Jackson, *Rejoice With Me*, Christian Courier Publications (2007) 36

be just vain repetition if we thoughtlessly repeated our thankfulness all day (Matthew 6:5-8). Conversely, ingratitude is a deadly but common sin. Human beings tend to neglect giving God proper gratitude let alone being excessively thankful. In Romans 1:20-21, Paul reveals it is evident that a lack of thankfulness revealed an evil heart of man that would reject the truth about God and worship created things.

There is something appealing, both psychologically and spiritually, about a man who has a humble heart that resembles the mind of Christ (2:5-8). James encourages us to be humble before God, and that then He will lift us up (James. 4:10). Humility is one of the prized characteristics as God sees it. It is said of Moses by the Lord that he was *"Moses my servant,"* rather than *"Moses my leader."* He was noted as the "meekest" (humble) of all who lived in his day (Numbers 12:3). It was also a quality of Jesus Christ (2 Corinthians 10:1).

With the Apostle Paul's example, we see that it is our duty to be thankful for each other on a constant basis. It is difficult to be upset with people while at the same time thanking God that they are our brothers or sisters in Christ. Thankfulness then can be offered in the form of a prayer and praise. Prayer and thanksgiving are almost inseparable, and they are most often offered together (1 Thessalonians 5:16-18).

Paul's letter to the Philippian church is something of a missionary thank you letter, but it is much more than that. It is the sharing of Paul's secret to experiencing Christian joy. At least 19 times in these four chapters, Paul mentions JOY, REJOICING, or GLADNESS. In spite of his danger and discomfort, Paul overflowed with joy. What was the secret of his joy? There is a difference in the concept of "happiness" and "joy." Happiness is dependent on circumstances, while joy is dependent on a relationship with Jesus Christ in spite of circumstances.

The secret to Paul's joy is found in another word: the word MIND; it is used 10 times by Paul and the word THINK is used 5 times in this book.

Experiencing Joy as a Choice

Have you ever stopped to consider how the circumstances of life are not really under our control? Weather, traffic, or what people say or do? The person whose happiness depends on ideal circumstances is going to be miserable much of the time. The poet Byron wrote, "Men are the sport of circumstances." Studies show that there are three things in our life that rob us of our joy:

1. Comparing ourselves with others
   (Galatians 6:4)
2. Worrying about things we can't control
   (Philippians 4:6, 7)
3. Trying to control things we shouldn't
   (1 Thessalonians 4:11)

All of us have lost our joy because of people sometime in our life. What they are, say, and do. We have probably also contributed to someone else's misery. But we have to live and work with people. Jesus said, *"A man's life consists not in the abundance of the things which he possesses"* (Luke 12:15). It is said that when dying (reported to be John Rockefeller), a very wealthy man, was asked what he wanted to make him happy before he died—he said, "Just a little more!"

The apostle Paul seemed to always be in the mindset of thankfulness. Of course, he had a lot to be thankful for. But we too often see our relationship with God as a relationship where God takes care of us and we are entitled. "Supplication" is to ask, to entreat God to supply; it is a specific type of prayer (1 Timothy 2:1). The apostle Paul prays with "Joy" (*charas*) even though he is in "bonds" (v. 7). It is that same disposition that Paul entertained a decade earlier in the Philippian jail as he and Silas sang hymns (Acts 16:25), and joy was still a constant companion. Paul tells us by inspiration that JOY is a choice. When he says that he has learned to be content (4:11), he means that he is choosing to not be a victim to his feelings or his environment. He is admonishing us to make the choice to be content, and we can be because of our relationship with Christ (4:13).

Two of the most respected Christian psychiatrists of the modern age, Drs. Frank Minirth, M.D., and Paul Meier, M.D., have written a book where they state,

> My associate and I have a combined post-high school education totaling over 30 years. During that time we thoroughly researched man's psychology, physiology, anatomy, mentality, and spirituality. We have also exercised our psychotherapeutic skills on thousands of patients. Both of us can say with a deep inner conviction that a majority of human beings do *not* have the inner peace and joy about which I am thinking. We are also convinced that all human beings are capable of having this inner joy and peace if only they will choose it and follow the right path to obtain it.[5]

---

[5] Paul Meier & Frank Minirth, *Happiness is a Choice*, Baker Books, (1978, 1994, 2007) 13

The Joy of Partnership in the Gospel

Paul thanks the Philippian Christians for their partnership (fellowship) in the gospel. The word "partnership" is translated from the Greek word *koinonia*, indicating partnership, participation with, or even financial sustenance (2 Corinthians 9:13) where the Greek term is rendered "contribution." Paul's thankful that the Philippian church did not allow things or comfort to rob them of their joy. They financially supported him in the proclamation of the gospel. The Philippians were a "mission-minded" church.

The fact that their fellowship is "in the gospel" is of great significance. Out of seventy-seven occurrences of the term "gospel" in the New Testament, sixty-three are to be found in the writings of Paul and in the Acts account of Paul's ministry. Philippians is a letter that is heavily weighted with a strong stress upon the saving message of the gospel.

Here Paul, early in the letter, introduces one of Christianity's most dynamic concepts: God's working in human lives. It has been astutely observed that in no other letter does he share his inner spirit-life so freely with his readers. This verse (vs. 6), with its stress on divine working in the Christian, touches the secret of Paul's own spiritual power. Christianity for Paul is a divine, human encounter in which the real dynamic for change is God Himself working in the Christian. Later in the letter Paul will say: *"for it is God who works in you both to will and to work, for his good pleasure"* (2:13). *"God is working in you,"* is a statement that probably most reflects the reason that Paul joyfully prays to the Lord. The Lord was his constant companion and he realized it most in his prayers and his work in the kingdom.

The Power of the Mind

We must be willing to accept the fact that the mind has the power to experience joy no matter what the circumstance might be. The power of the mind continues to amaze even the casual observer. The brain is much like a computer. It has access to a personal library of thousands of thoughts and pictures, ready to expose them on the imaginary monitor screen in our heads at a moment's notice. The mind can recall, at will, any programmed belief system that is in that personal library. Some of the belief systems are true and some are false.

The brain does amazing things but appears unable to distinguish the difference between a truth and a lie. If a person believes that something is true, the brain will accept it as truth. All that is required is repetition of that belief for the brain to record it as truth for all time. Just like a computer's hard drive, whatever you have saved in your mind will stay there until you change it.

Most belief systems are formed in our childhood. Once accepted, these beliefs are recorded as true even if they are not. *Belief Systems* then, are those collections of beliefs that the brain has recorded (after much repetition) and recalls at will because we use them when needed and believe them to be true. These belief systems have a direct relationship to how we see our world and how we think our world sees us.

The apostle Paul established this concept as God ordained when he said, *"Do not conform any longer to the pattern of this world, but be transformed by the renewing of your mind"* (Romans 12:2). The Bible emphasizes that we should control our thoughts and imaginations (Philippians 4:8). Paul says that we should control our thoughts and bring them into the captivity of Jesus Christ. He states,

We demolish arguments and every pretension that sets itself up against the knowledge of God, and we take captive every thought to make it obedient to Christ (2 Corinthians 10:5).

These belief systems create in us a potential series of *perceived threats* that we allow to control our feelings and behavior. Even if the belief systems are lies, if we believe them to be true, they can be acted upon as true and become *self-destructive lies* that cause us to make wrong choices that lead to sin in our lives.

These belief systems then cause us to perceive things as threats, whether real or imaginary, and threats cause us to get angry. In reality, **all anger is a response to a perceived threat**. Since anger is a defense mechanism, we then react to perceived threats automatically, often causing a lot of heartaches and problems in our interpersonal relationships. Reactions to perceived threats are automatic and programmed in our subconscious mind. We learned such automatic reactions to threats from the angry behavior of significant people in our lives when we were children and because certain temperaments are prone to different anger responses. We usually do not challenge these responses. They become automatic like driving a car.

There is also a danger in programming our minds to pursue pleasure or happiness rather than doing what is *right*, because it might involve suffering or inconvenience. If parents emphasize *truth seeking* rather than *happiness seeking*, the child will be more willing to accept the trials and difficulties in life with a sense of endurance that will provide strength and tolerance that builds character.

Many of us grew up either reading or knowing about the philosophy of "thinking positive thoughts will bring about positive results." There was a book written many years ago that still has a psychological hold on people's minds even today. Dr. Norman Vincent Peale, a minister and author, wrote the book *The Power of Positive Thinking*, which focuses on the positive and ignores the negative. It is a philosophy that many non-believers have espoused that says in reality, "I can pick myself up by my own bootstraps if I just think good, positive thoughts."

The problem with *positive thinking* as a philosophy is that it creates a positive filtering in our minds, which then leads to denial and distortion of reality. Those who filter out reality, whether positively or negatively, think inaccurately and end up misinterpreting themselves and others. It is a belief that says, "I can save myself." It is a belief system that in essence portrays a mindset of not needing God or anyone else in our lives to direct us or empower us. It is a philosophy that coincides with the belief that there is no absolute truth, and that we can become a law unto ourselves. Instead of engaging in *positive thinking*, we need to teach our children and ourselves to develop the skill of *truth thinking*. For it is not positive thinking that saves us and makes us free; it is the truth of God's Word (John 7:17; 8:32).

Carson McCullers, the novelist, was described at her death as having a "vocation of pain." "Much of her art," a critic related, "seemed to have flowed from her own tortured life." Before she was 29, Mrs. McCullers had suffered three strokes that paralyzed her left side. Discouraged, she was sure that she could never write again. Eventually she resumed her work, writing a page a day. However, her pain increased in her later years. Her husband committed suicide, and illness left her a virtual cripple. In a rare mention of her troubles, she said, "Sometimes I think God got me mixed up with Job. But Job never cursed God, and neither have I. I carry on."[6]

---

[6] Taken from a periodical: Dynamic Preaching, (October, 1992) 17, 18

Sharing in God's Glory Requires Suffering

Paul reminds us of the reality of the Christian's suffering for the cause of Christ. He says,

Now if we are children, then we are heirs–heirs of God and co-heirs with Christ, if indeed we share in his sufferings in order that we may also share in his glory (Romans 8:17).

In God's scheme of things, suffering as a Christian is a prerequisite to experiencing the glory He has for us.

If we have the mindset of trusting God in all things, and believing the teachings of the Bible that suffering is a good and positive thing and that we will grow from it, we will be able to rejoice in our sufferings and joyfully thank God in all of our prayers. But we must develop the belief system through prayer and repetition that programs the subconscious mind to accept suffering and inconvenience as valuable tools for correction and discipline in our Christian walk; for *"we live by faith, not by sight"* (2 Corinthians 5:7).

Albert Lemmons writes in his wonderful book on prayer and fasting,

> Deep in the heart of many Christians is the admission that their prayer life lacks the power they desire. When we are old, we will have achieved much more than now and there won't be any questions about the role of God in your heart and in your life. The true purpose of prayer is to enable one to set the power of God to work in his life; to overcome problems and difficulties and to be

utilized fully in the Master's service.[7]

Such a motivation, as true disciples, should promote in our hearts a sense of JOY when facing trials, suffering and struggles in our lives.

The author, Tony Campolo, tells a story about a friend of his who had to take a bus trip across central India. He states,

> He was in one of those old-model buses that should have been retired a decade ago; it was seemingly held together with string and glue. As is often the case with buses in Third World countries, this bus was packed, not only with people, but with packages, furniture, and just about every kind of domesticated animal.

He went on to say,

> Sitting across the aisle was a very tired man whose neatly wrapped package sat on the luggage rack over his head. The old man wanted to yield to the sleepiness that was threatening to overtake him, but he couldn't for fear that while he was asleep, someone might take his package. As he rode along, the old man would doze off from time to time. Each time that happened, he would wake with a sense of terror that his package might be stolen. He would quickly jerk his head sideways so he might check things out and make sure the package was still there. That went on for hours. Then as the man snapped out of one of his tense and momentary catnaps, he

---

[7] Albert G. Lemmons, *Prayer and Fasting*, Williamstown Bible College Press, (1978) 24

looked up to find that his precious package was gone. Momentary panic crossed the old man's face as he realized he had been robbed. Then he smiled to himself, leaned back in his seat, totally relaxed, and fell into a prolonged and delicious sleep. Being relieved of the thing that had caused him constant nervousness, he had enough sense to enjoy being unencumbered.[8]

Compolo adds that not many of us are that smart.

Is it not true that many of us are constantly looking at our packages and life becomes more burdensome than it needs to be, and our joy is weakened and our desire to serve Jesus becomes less a priority. The apostle Paul said it this way, *"But whatever was to my profit I now consider loss for the sake of Christ"* (3:7).

Avon Malone states,

This Philippian letter may well illustrate the thanksgiving at its loveliest among the inspired letters of the New Testament. Paul had a genius for friendship, and there was a perpetual geyser of gratitude in his heart. With great warmth he expresses his affectionate appreciation for his Philippian friends. Every memory of them is a grateful remembrance. Every supplication on their behalf is a joyful one. The language of verse does not demand that we understand that the Philippians were always mentioned each time Paul prayed. Paul is rather saying that each time he did make

---

[8] Tony Campolo, *Carpe Diem*, Word Publishing, 1994, 222

supplication for them, it was joyfully done.[9]

The Great Creator

God is the great Designer of all things. He especially designed man to be holy, righteous, compassionate, and joyful. Those who reject God as the great Designer of man's soul have nowhere to turn for a source of peace and joy. The idea of being joyful in life, even when facing trials and temptations, is foreign to the man of the world, the non-believer. When you know the "Who," the answer to the rest of the question, "who am I and where am I going," is no longer a dilemma. Faith is responsible for such reasoning, not human logic.

The story is told that Sir Isaac Newton believed the Bible and was a Christian, according to his writings. He made a replica of our solar system in miniature. In the center was the sun with all the planets revolving around it in their various proximities. A scientist entered Newton's study one day and exclaimed, "My!" "What an exquisite thing this is!" "Who made it?" "Nobody," replied Newton to the questioner, who was an unbeliever. "You must think I am a fool." "Of course somebody made it, and he is a genius." Laying aside his book, Newton arose and laid a hand on his friend's shoulder and said:

> This thing is but a puny imitation of a much grander system whose laws you and I know, and I am not able to convince you that this mere toy is without a designer and maker; yet you profess to believe that the great original from which the design is taken has come into being without either designer or maker. Now tell me, by what sort of reasoning do you reach

---

[9] Avon Malone, *Press to the Prize*, 21st Century Christian, 25

such incongruous conclusions?[10]

We human creatures are so very strange. We will believe almost anything except what millions of people have based their lives on over the past two thousand years. And that is that the God of the universe is available through prayer.

There have been reports over the years of the so-called SETI project–the Search for Extra Terrestrial Intelligence. From the late 1960's until 1993, NASA funded this effort to one degree or another. Since 1993, the effort has been supported by the private non-profit SETI Institute and the grassroots SETI League.

For 45 years, spending hundreds of millions of dollars, we have been sending messages into the universe with the purpose of discovering whether there is any other intelligent life out there. And there has not been one response. Not one.

Yet you and I can kneel down anywhere on earth and communicate with the One who created this universe and everything that is in it. Why in the world do we not make use of this amazing resource? That is why the apostle Paul speaks of JOYFULLY thanking God in prayer.

---

[10] Dynamic Preaching, (May 1992) 91

Questions for Review

1. How would you define the concept of "Joy?"
2. What is the difference between the concept of "happiness" and "joy?"
3. Why is "joyfully thanking God in our prayers" so important?
4. What is the harm in promoting "Positive Thinking?"
5. How would you prove that JOY is a choice?
6. What is the power of the mind?
7. Why does God require suffering in our Christian walk?
8. How do we know that Paul is in prison?

Lesson Two
(Chapter 1:7-11)

Joyfully Claiming Holiness in Christ

It is right for me to feel this way about all of you, since I have you in my heart; for whether I am in chains or defending and confirming the gospel, all of you share in God's grace with me. God can testify how I long for all of you with the affection of Christ Jesus.

And this is my prayer: that your love may abound more and more in knowledge and depth of insight, so that you may be able to discern what is best and may be pure and blameless until the day of Christ, filled with the fruit of righteousness that comes through Jesus Christ–to the glory and praise of God.

Michael Yaconelli, in his book, *Dangerous Wonder: The Adventure of Childlike Faith*, says,

> The most critical issue facing Christians in this age is not abortion, pornography, the disintegration of the family, moral relativity, MTV, drugs, racism, sexuality, or school prayer. The critical issue today is *dullness*. We have lost our astonishment. The Good News is no longer *good* news, it is *okay* news. Christianity is no longer life *changing*, it is life *enhancing*. Jesus doesn't change people into *wild-eyed radicals* anymore; he changes them into *nice people*.

Yaconelli is right in his assessment of modern day Christianity. The apostle Paul would probably not recognize the so-called Christian church today. He would most likely be astonished at our pursuit of happiness over truth. The prophet James also would be astonished at what he would see that is described as Christianity. We have a tendency to overlook James admonition when he says,

> *Consider it pure joy, my brothers, whenever you face trials of many kinds, because you know that the testing of your faith develops perseverance. Perseverance must finish its work so that you may be mature and complete, not lacking anything* (James 1:2-4).

James is showing us that when trials, temptations, or unwanted experiences come into our lives, we must look beyond them to the victory we will enjoy by working through them. When passing through such trials, we hardly find them joyful, but when they are passed, we realize the power of God has helped us through these trials, and we find it joyful, because of the victory.

Happiness Seeking vs. Truth Seeking

As Christians, how should we face the difficult circumstances of life, which at times are harsh and unyielding? James says in chapter one verse two, "consider it," which comes from the Greek word *hegesasthe*, which has to do with our internal attitude of the mind that causes the circumstances of life to affect us unfavorably or constructively.[11] Another thought about the word *hegesasthe*, will help us to see the wisdom of the Spirit when He inspired James to write the book. We face pressures from without and within. How do we cope with them? The word can be translated, "think forward, consider." James is saying that, as we live in the present we should think forward to the future. We may face some kind of *cross* now, but the *crown* and *glory* will come to us. Pushed about by men now, but then reigning with Christ in our heavenly home. The future rewards of the Christian will drive out the darkness of the present. That is how Christ could face the cross and its pain and humiliation with *joy* (Hebrews 12:2).

James further says in his dissertation on facing trials with *joy*, that if this is too much for you to understand, then ask God for the wisdom to understand it. In other words, let the Lord help you find the joy that can be experienced as you face trials knowing that the future result will be growth in faith, security, peace, tranquility, maturity and holiness.

> *If any of you lacks wisdom, he should ask God, who gives generously to all without finding fault, and it will be given to him. But when he asks, he must believe and not doubt, because he who doubts is like a wave of the sea, blown and tossed by the wind. That man should not think he will receive anything from the Lord; he is a double-minded man, unstable in all he does* (James 1:5-8).

This kind of faith is not based on the HAPPINESS of circumstances, but on the JOY that is based on a trust in Christ Jesus. Such wisdom transcends the wisdom of the

---

[11] A. T. Robertson; *Word Pictures in the New Testament*, General Epistles, Baker Book House, 1933.

world, because it is counter-cultural, if you please. It is based on the priority of TRUTH SEEKING, rather than HAPPINESS SEEKING. The apostle Peter also tells us that,

> *...through the resurrection of Jesus Christ from the dead, and into an inheritance that can never perish, spoil or fade–kept in heaven for you, who through faith are shielded by God's power until the coming of the salvation that is ready to be revealed in the last time. In this you greatly rejoice, though now for a little while you may have had to suffer grief in all kinds of trials. These have come so that your faith–of greater worth than gold, which perishes even though refined by fire–may be proved genuine and may result in praise, glory and honor when Jesus Christ is revealed* (1 Peter 1:4-7).

Do we not see that Peter is confirming what the other apostles, prophets, and Jesus Himself have said, that through suffering and trials our holiness is tested and proven to be the quality that is necessary to experience the resurrection and eternity with Christ.

The problem today is that our young people have bought into the philosophy that they are entitled to happiness. There is this concept in America, probably because of our wealth, that parents have the responsibility of providing *happiness* in their lives as an entitlement because they are children. Therefore, they feel that their "needs" must be met. Their gratification is priority one. In America today, many have lost the capacity to suffer, be uncomfortable, or simply endure not having their so-called needs go unmet.

An article in "Think Magazine," edited by Dr. Brad Harrab, entitled, *The Perils of McParenting*, states,

Today's society seems to be geared toward short-term, quick fixes of problems and situations instead of long-range character building when it comes to parenting. There are hundreds of parenting styles: experimental parenting, default parenting, friendship parenting, and the list goes on. Due to these inconsistent and ungodly parenting styles, we are creating homes of havoc, difficulty and stress which develop the attitude of 'I can't wait until my children are grown and out on their own!'[12]

In other words, the concept of holiness is totally foreign to most young people today. It represents the idea of "holier than thou," or "goodie two-shoes," or "self-righteous," or "perfection," or "sinless," or "sainthood." None of these stereotypes are correct. But when people are engaged in *happiness seeking* as an entitlement, their belief systems are beyond understanding the truth of the concept of *holiness*. Yet for the Christian, there is no other way to achieve eternal life.

It is interesting that the apostle Paul adds, in this segment of Philippians, that they were partakers with him in "grace." Wayne Jackson states,

> In the Greek text, 'grace' is accompanied by the article, thus, 'the grace.' This may denote the system of grace, i.e., the gospel plan, in which they were to have a common experience. Or, it may suggest that God had granted the Philippians a 'favor,' in allowing them to *suffer* with Paul as they labored together for the cause of Christ. It is sometimes hard for us to digest the fact that it is a privilege to suffer for Christ, but that is the teaching of the Scriptures.[13]

---

[12] Steve Minor, *The Perils of McParenting*, Think Magazine, July 2011
[13] Jackson, 40

The Power of Holiness

Holiness is not a very popular concept in our world today. The word "holiness" comes from the Greek word *hagios*, which "fundamentally signifies separated and hence, in Scripture in its moral and spiritual significance, separated from sin and therefore, consecrated to God, sacred."[14]

Frequently, we think of holiness as having to do with those things which we must do to be holy. But this is only one aspect of holiness. Along with this definition, is the thought that we must be lights unto the world (Matthew 5:14-16). We may even shy away from the idea of holiness because of the connotation of "holier than thou" and the implication of spiritual arrogance. To understand holiness properly, we must begin not with ourselves, but with God, whose essential nature is holiness. The apostle Peter said,

> *As obedient children, do not conform to the evil desires you had when you lived in ignorance. But just as he who called you is holy, so be holy in all you do; for it is written: 'Be holy, because I am holy'* (1 Peter 1:14-16).

Holiness as applied to God describes His "differentness," His "uniqueness." He is the one who is all that we are not and who exists in utter perfection.

The Christians to whom the book of Hebrews was originally written were in grave danger of giving up their faith in Christ and reverting to their former Jewish religion. Apparently as a result of discouragement, persecution, and a failure to appreciate the uniqueness of their Savior, they were contemplating trading their new faith for the old one. We are

---

[14] Vines, 566

not only called to be holy, our holiness is absolutely imperative. The Hebrew writer states, *"Make every effort to live in peace with all men and to be holy; without holiness no one will see the Lord"* (Hebrews 12:14). To fail to obtain holiness is to fail to obtain the grace of God.

The book of Hebrews also reflects the discipline of God. Holiness does not come easy for any of us. Our sinful nature is so far from God's holy nature that considerable refinement is required. In ways which we may not realize, we are lacking in the holiness which God requires. In Hebrews 12:3-11, the writer addresses his readers' situation of experiencing persecution. He describes this, not as an unfortunate circumstance by which his readers were being victimized, but as the "discipline of the Lord."

The author compares the discipline which we receive from our earthly fathers to that of our heavenly Father. The former disciplined us temporarily "at their pleasure," that is, as they saw fit, whether right or wrong. But God's discipline, he says, *"trains us for our good, that we may share in HIS HOLINESS"* (Hebrews 12:10). Even Jesus learned obedience from what He suffered (Hebrews 5:8).

Thus Paul is praying that the church may be pure and blameless, so that we may obtain the holiness of God. It is evident according to the Scriptures that we cannot obtain such holiness without the blood of Christ cleansing us and without the discipline that only suffering and hardship can prepare us for. If we have the mindset of happiness seeking, of avoiding inconvenience and difficulty at all costs, we will not be disciplined enough to develop such holiness. And the Hebrew writer tells us it is imperative that we have the holiness of Jesus Christ in order to obtain eternal life.

God's Life Insurance Policy

God does not allow us to simply coast through life. Coasting through life without growing in holiness is exactly what Satan wants us to do. He knows that we will weaken and fall if we try to simply maintain our status quo. The idea of transformation requires change. And it is a daily change, requiring us to grow in the knowledge and love of our Lord. The apostle Peter put it this way:

> *For this very reason, make every effort to add to your faith goodness; and to goodness, knowledge; and to knowledge, self-control; and to self-control, perseverance; and to perseverance, godliness; and to godliness, brotherly kindness; and to brotherly kindness, love. For if you possess these qualities in* ***increasing measure****, they will keep you from being ineffective and unproductive in your knowledge of our Lord Jesus Christ. But if anyone does not have them, he is nearsighted and blind, and has forgotten that he has been cleansed from his past sins. Therefore, my brothers, be all the more eager to make your calling and election sure. For if you do these things, you will never fall, and you will receive a rich welcome into the eternal kingdom of our Lord and Savior Jesus Christ* (2 Peter 1:5-11).

What a life insurance policy that is! Growing in holiness is the key. We must be willing to confess our own neediness, our struggles and problems–even our sins. We are not called together as the body of Christ because we are paragons of righteousness, not because we are 'okay.' And because we aren't, we need the Lord and each other. But in most churches, such honesty about self seldom occurs. Few of us want to allow ourselves to be seen as we really are. What would people think, if they knew the truth about my marriage? My children? My temptations? My frustrations? My doubts? My fears? And so we hide our real selves and then wonder why we feel so empty, so alone, even in the midst of the family of God! This is tragic, because the very truthfulness we so studiously avoid has the power to set us free.[15]

It seems that the Bible is telling us that we must be holy as Jesus Christ is holy and the only way to achieve such character is to be totally transformed into the likeness of Jesus Christ (Ephesians 4:20-24). Paul talks about the transformation into the likeness of Jesus as an ongoing process in our daily walk with Him. In 2 Corinthians 3:18, the Greek text is in the present tense, reflecting a progressive process for all time. The Greek word translated "transformed" is *metamorphoo*, from which we get the word "metamorphosis," which means, "to change into another form," such as the caterpillar changes into the butterfly. It is a change that is complete and ongoing; not an incremental change of small portions, but one of significance, in other words, one that is life–changing (Romans 12:2). It is a change that must be based on our *hope* in Jesus Christ. The apostle John said it this way: *"Everyone who has this hope in him purifies himself, just as he is pure"* (1 John 3:3).

The Agape Principle

Jackson states,

> There is a tremendously important point here (v.9). 'Love,' as a mere sentimental, unguided emotion, is not a virtue applauded in the Scriptures. Love must be

---

[15] Tommy South, *That We May Share His Holiness*, Bible Guides, 40

educated. According to the apostle, love must grow within the channels of knowledge and discernment.[16]

Jesus Christ sets the standard for us to love one another as He has loved us (John 13:34, 35). Jesus also said that if you love Him, you will keep His commandments (John 14:15).

The Agape Principle requires of us that we love our neighbor regardless of what he/she believes or how he/she behaves towards us (Matthew 19:19). *Agape* is the noun form of the Greek word for "unconditional love." When Jesus said, *"Love your neighbor as yourself,"* He used this word (*agapao*–verb form) in this passage when describing how we should love our neighbor. *Phileo* is the verb form in the Greek for "affectionate love." *Phileo* is not normally used as a command to love someone. *Agapao* can be commanded because it is a type of love that doesn't require *emotional attachment*, much like JOY can be commanded because it is a choice. It is a choice that the mind can make if it is trained by repetition to believe that we can make that choice.

When speaking of how *agapao* is used in reference to God (1 John 4:9-10), W. E. Vine says, "But obviously this is not the love of complacency, or affection, that is, it was not drawn out by an excellency in its objects."[17]

That's how Jesus could love us and command us to love and serve our enemies (Matthew 5:44-48; Romans 5:8; 12:17-21; 13:9). "Agape Love" is a proactive love that requires action.

A good biblical definition of *agape love* would be, "the kind of love that does not require affection, but does require that we make a choice to do what is best for someone even if

---

[16] Jackson, 43
[17] Vine's, 382

he/she doesn't like it or thinks that it is unloving." As Christians, God expects us to love everyone unconditionally, whether we like them or not.

Thus Paul is praying that agape love will abound in us as Christians and that it is a *choice* that depends on the right mindset and it is based on truth. Therefore, *truth seeking* is more important than *happiness seeking*. Happiness seeking will always disappoint us eventually, but truth seeking will mold and train us in righteousness and holiness. There is nothing wrong with wanting to find *happiness* in your life, but it should not be at the expense of obeying the truth of God's Word. Jesus puts truth seeking above happiness seeking when it comes to family or loved ones (Matthew 10:34-39).

Barclay says of love,

> Love is always the way to knowledge. If we love any subject, we want to learn more about it; if we love someone, we want to learn more about that person; if we love Jesus, we will want to learn more about him and about his truth.[18]

Malone states,

> This kind of love will solve the 'Euodia–Syntche' (4:2) problems of the first century and the twentieth century. It is the panacea for the pettiness that sometimes divides God's children.[19]

---

[18] William Barclay, *The Letters to the Philippians, Colossians, and Thessalonians*, The New Daily Study Bible, Westminster Press, 22

[19] Malone, 31

The Single Mind

In spite of his difficult circumstances as a prisoner in Rome, Paul is rejoicing. The secret of JOY is the *single mind*; Paul lives for Christ and the gospel. *Christ* is named 18 times in chapter one and *gospel* 6 times. So what really is the "single mind?" It is the attitude that says, "It makes no difference what happens to me, just as long as Christ is glorified and the gospel is shared with others."

Paul says, *"I have you in my heart."* It is possible to have others in our minds without really having them in our hearts. Paul's sincere love for his friends was something that could not be disguised or hidden. JOY is "internal" not "external," and HAPPINESS is an elusive pursuit. How did Paul evidence his love for them? He was suffering on their behalf. His bonds were proof of his love. He was a *"prisoner of Jesus Christ for you Gentiles"* (Ephesians 3:1). Paul prays that they might experience abounding and discerning love. He also prays that they might develop a mature Christian character, and that they might experience Christian service.

Again, James reminds us that a double–minded man is unstable and a vacillating person who cannot expect to be blessed by God (James. 1:6). The term "double-minded" is an interesting word. It comes from the Greek word *dipsuchos*, and it literally means, "two-souled, one personality, but two souls." He is the man who can't make up his mind as to who he will follow. He is much like the Rich Young Ruler of Matthew 19, who asked Jesus what he lacked, and when told he should give all that he had to the poor, he rejected the sage advice of the Lord, and walked away. He wanted to be saved, but he didn't want to give up his worldly possessions to do so. He is the opposite of the single-minded man, who puts his hand to the plow and never looks back (Luke 9:62).

Joyfully Claiming Holiness in Christ

The single-minded man presses on toward the goal of taking hold of Christ Jesus. Paul describes it this way when he says, *"But whatever was to my profit I now consider loss for the sake of Christ"* (3:7). We make choices every day, and we so often choose to be unhappy because of what somebody said or did to us. Yet we could have chosen not to get angry or sad, etc., and made the choice to remain content. Someone said,

> You can take a piece of wax, a piece of meat, some sand, some clay, and some wood shavings and put them on the fire and see how they react. Each of them is being acted upon by the same agent; yet, the wax melts, the meat fries, the sand dries up, the clay hardens, and the shavings burn up. Just so, under the identical influence of circumstances and environment, one man is made better, one man becomes stronger, another weaker, another hardened about life, another very angry, and another withers away.

This explains why one hears the Word of God and is made better, while another is made bitter. "Choices"– it's our responsibility to decide how we are going to react to what life throws at us. The apostle Paul made some choices about life also, and he said, *"Rejoice in the Lord always, I will say again: Rejoice! ...for I have learned to be content whatever the circumstances"* (4:4, 11).

In his memoirs about surviving the World War II concentration camps, Elie Wiesel claims,

> He needed to stay alive to take care of his elderly father. That became his motivation for surviving the concentration camps. He says that he knew that if he died, his father would give up hope and die also.

Weisel wrote,

> The Germans tried to get the inmates to think only of themselves, to forget relatives and friends, to tend only to their own needs. But what happened was just the reverse. Those who retreated to a universe limited to their own bodies had less chance of getting out alive, while to live for a brother, a friend, an ideal, helped you hold out longer.[20]

For the Christian, having a *single mind* empowers him to focus on his life in Christ and to be able to "walk by faith." It allows him to direct all his energies on his purpose as a Christian and empowers him to joyfully claim holiness in Christ.

Being Blameless

Paul states that the ultimate goal of a Christian is to be sincere (NASV) and blameless until the day of Christ (1:10). Barclay says that the Greek word for "sincere" is *eilikrines*;

> It may come from *eile*, which means sunshine, and *krinein*, which means to judge. It may, therefore, describe that which is able to stand the test of the sunshine; that which can be exposed to the sun, held up to the light of the sun, without any flaw appearing. If that be the meaning of the word, it means that the Christian character can stand any light that is turned upon it. But *eilikrines* may be derived from *eilein*, which means to whirl round and round, as in a sieve and so to sift until every

---

[20] Elie Wiesel, *All Rivers Run to The Sea*

impurity is extracted. If that is the meaning, it means that the Christian character is cleansed and sifted of all evil until it is altogether pure.[21]

Jackson adds in reference to 'filled with the fruit of righteousness' (1:11);

> 'Being filled' (*pepleromenoi*) is a perfect tense, passive voice form. The perfect tense reveals the abiding state of their spiritual activity, yet the passive voice suggests that the fruits are not the result of meritorious accomplishment. These fruits are the consequence of the working of Christ in the Christian's submissive life. The ultimate goal of this fervent activity, of course, is the 'glory and praise of God.' For what other reason does man exist?[22]

---

[21] Barclay, 23
[22] Jackson; 43, 44

Questions for Review

1. What is the meaning of the concept of holiness?
2. What is the meaning of the Agape Principle?
3. Describe God's Life Insurance Policy.
4. What does the Single Mind refer to?
5. How would you define the Greek word *Agape*?
6. How would you define the Greek word *Phileo*?
7. Define the Greek word *hegesasthe*.
8. How would you describe the concept of Being Blameless?

Lesson Three
(Chapter 1:12-26)

Joyfully Facing the Unexpected

Now I want you to know, brothers that what has happened to me has really served to advance the gospel. As a result, it has become clear throughout the whole palace guard and to everyone else that I am in chains for Christ. Because of my chains, most of the brothers in the Lord have been encouraged to speak the word of God more courageously and fearlessly.

It is true that some preach Christ out of envy and rivalry, but others out of goodwill. The latter do so in love, knowing that I am put here for the defense of the gospel. The former preach Christ out of selfish ambition, not sincerely, supposing that they can stir up trouble for me while I am in chains. But what does it matter? The important thing is that in every way, whether from false motives or true, Christ is preached. And because of this I rejoice.

Yes, and I will continue to rejoice, for I know that through your prayers and the help given by the Spirit of Jesus Christ, what has happened to me will turn out for my deliverance. I eagerly expect and hope that I will in no way be ashamed, but will have sufficient courage so that now as always Christ will be exalted in my body, whether by life or by death. For to me, to live is Christ and to die is gain. If I am to go on living in the body, this will mean fruitful labor for me. Yet what shall I choose? I do not know! I am torn between the two: I desire to depart and be with Christ, which is better by far; but it is more necessary for you that I remain in the body. Convinced of this, I know that I will remain, and I will continue with all of you for your progress and joy in the faith, so that through my being with you again your joy in Christ Jesus will overflow on account of me.

The following notice appeared in a newspaper in the northeastern part of the United States:

> To those of you, who bought our book *Skydiving Made Easy*, please enter the following correction on page 12, paragraph 3, line 2. The words *state zip code*, should say *pull rip cord*. We regret any inconvenience this mistake may have caused you.

Most, if not all of us, do not like to experience surprises that we are not prepared for and affect our welfare. The apostle Paul knew that a possible imprisonment was ahead of him, but he seems somewhat surprised that it would be in Rome to the extent that it would hinder his ministry as an apostle. Paul is joyfully surprised that his imprisonment is benefitting his ministry. In verse 12 of this chapter, Paul is impressed with the *advance* of the gospel while he is in prison. The term "advance" in the NIV is from the Greek word *prokope*, derived from *pro*, "forward" and *kopto*, "to cut."[23] Originally the word was used

---

[23] Vine's, 35

of a pioneer cutting his way through the wilderness. Paul is saying that his imprisonment is *cutting the way*, for the gospel being preached to a wider audience than perhaps Paul could have reached otherwise.

To Paul's credit, he wasn't looking for happiness in his ministry, but to please God. The whole realm of happiness seeking affects every facet of our lives, when it becomes a quest. For instance in marriage, happiness seeking is detrimental to the peace and tranquility of a husband and wife becoming one flesh as God so designed. Cloud and Townsend, in their insightful book on marriage state,

> I can't think of a worse value in life, especially a life that includes marriage. Why? Is this a killjoy attitude? Hardly. I am not advocating misery. I hate pain. But I do know this: *People who always want to be happy and pursue it above all else are some of the most miserable people in the world.*
>
> The reason is that happiness is a result. It is sometimes the result of having good things happen. But usually it is the result of our being in a good place inside ourselves and our having done the character work we need to do so that we are content and joyful in whatever circumstance we find ourselves. Happiness is a fruit of a lot of hard work in relationships, career, spiritual growth, or a host of other arenas of life. But nowhere is this as true as in marriage.[24]

---

[24] Henry Cloud & John Townsend, *Boundaries in Marriage*, Zondervan, 109-110

The Vision of an All-Powerful God

Rabbi Harold Kushner wrote a best-selling book, *When Bad Things Happen to Good People*. He wrote this book after watching his young son, Aaron, suffer from one of the most heart-wrenching conditions which a human being can confront. The boy had *progeria*, a disease in which the aging process is bizarrely speeded up. Kushner was told that Aaron would never have any hair or grow over three feet tall. At six years of age he would have the skin and bone structure of an old man. Harold Kushner watched his son shrivel up, grow weak, and finally die, all before his fifteenth birthday. Can you imagine anything more horrible?

In his book, Kushner said he grew to accept God's love, but question God's power. He says he came to believe that God is good, and hates to see people suffer, but is not powerful enough to solve all the world's problems. God is all loving, but not all-powerful.

The question is can we be sympathetic to his solution? Kushner's book was a best seller because many people find this solution appealing. We believe God loves us, yet we still hurt; so is the belief that God's power is limited the only possible alternative? Yet, if you believe in Christ, which I do, then we see that God is all-powerful when we examine the resurrection of Christ.

The main problem with this kind of thinking is Scripture. The testimony of Scripture is that God is both all-loving and all-powerful. Philip Yancey asks the question in his book, *Where Is God When It Hurts?*

> Why didn't God reveal this truth, that God's power is limited, to Job, if it is the truth? Job had just about every disaster imaginable befall him. Why didn't God say to Job, 'Sorry, Job. I did the best I

could. You know how it is.' Instead, Job 38-41 contains one of the most impressive descriptions of God's power that you will find anywhere. For the Christian community the concept of a limited God is simply unacceptable. It is clearly unbiblical.

The apostle Paul believed in the all powerful God of the Bible. He said to the Corinthians,

When I came to you, brothers, I did not come with eloquence or superior wisdom as I proclaimed to you the testimony about God. For I resolved to know nothing while I was with you except Jesus Christ and him crucified. I came to you in weakness and fear, and with much trembling. My message and my preaching were not with wise and persuasive words, but with a demonstration of the Spirit's power, so that your faith might not rest on men's wisdom, but on God's power (1 Corinthians 2:1-5).

The strength of Paul's leadership rests on his vision of an all-powerful God.

Many Christians are attracted by a leader's personality and charisma. Followers, on the other hand, are attracted by the leader's vision. Followers want to be challenged by great goals. They want to commit to something larger than themselves. Among the crowds, who came to see Jesus preach and teach, many were fans but only a few were true followers.[25]

---

[25] Randy Frazee, *The Comeback Congregation*, Abingdon Press, 1995, 16

To begin with, these chains gave Paul contact with the lost. He even converted some who were of Caesar's household (4:22). The secret is that if you have the single mind, you look upon your circumstances as God-given opportunities for the furthering of the gospel. Paul is rejoicing at "what God is going to do," rather than regretting what God did not do. Paul refused to let circumstances rob him of his joy, and he also gave courage to the saved (1:14).

For those of us who are adults, one thing that makes Christmas so joyful is seeing the wide-eyed expressions of wonder on little faces. Children know about *joy*. Adults can lose their joy so easily. What does it take to rob you of your *joy*? What causes more holiday headaches, someone asked: a household of relatives or the words "some assembly required"? The Exedrin Headache Resource Center took a poll to find out. Here is a list of the *joy robbers* they discovered during the holiday season:

1. Fighting crowds and traffic
2. Not getting enough sleep and changing sleep patterns
3. Not having enough time to get everything done
4. Spending too much money
5. Eating or drinking too much
6. Skipping meals because of busy schedule
7. Getting together with friends and family
8. Cooking and cleaning
9. Long plane/train/car trips
10. Being apart from friends and family during the holidays[26]

Paul stays consistent with his values when he doesn't allow the circumstances of opposing critics rob him of his joy. It is hard to believe that anyone would oppose Paul in the

---

[26] Newsweek, *Holiday Pain*, December 18, 1995, 8

church. Paul says that some preached Christ sincerely, some out of jealousy. But again, he doesn't let circumstances destroy his contentment in Christ (4:11).

Motives for Preaching

Malone reminds us that

> A sobering lesson becomes apparent: it is possible to do right things out of wrong motives. Paul does not rejoice in the wrong *motive* of those who preach out of envy and strife; he rejoices in the *message*. The great, magnanimous heart of the apostle exults that Christ is preached. That message will save regardless of the motive of the messenger. However, caution is needed here lest one conclude that motive is unimportant. Motive is crucially important to that one holding the motive. It is not the suffering but the motive that makes the martyr.[27]

The principle that Paul lays down is this: *"God must work in us before He can work through us"* (2:13). This principle is seen at work in the lives of men like Moses, David, and the apostles. Moses needed 40 years of tending sheep and God working with him to prepare him for his work. Paul in Arabia, and David as a shepherd are examples of the time and patience it took for God to train capable men.

After Paul's conversion, he makes Jesus Christ the center of his life. The words: *"For to me, to live is Christ and to die is gain,"* tells the whole story of why Paul

---

[27] Malone, 38

continues to preach the gospel (1:21). He did not live for personal gain, or prosperity. The single purpose in his life was to serve Christ. Paul did not want to bring shame on the name of Christ, either in life or death. In reference to Paul's imprisonment Gordon Fee says,

> Thus if Paul is released as he expects, he will continue (now as always) in full pursuit of knowing Christ and making him known. Likewise, if he is executed, the goal of living has thus been reached: he will finally have gained Christ... This expressed not a death wish, not dissatisfaction with life, nor desire to be done with troubles and trials; it is the forthright assessment of one whose immediate future is somewhat uncertain but whose ultimate future is both certain and to be desired... Such a statement, of course, has meaning only for one to whom the first clause is a vibrant, living reality. Otherwise death is a *loss* or *gain* only in the sense of escape. [28]

It is evident that Paul knew that he could be executed at any time. His desire to live longer is related to his desire to give more service to Christ.

> Paul's statement; *'to die is gain,'* is one of the classic texts of the New Testament. Phillips renders the first clause: 'Living to me simply means Christ.' Remove Christ from Paul's life and there is nothing left! Jesus Christ is the totality of life to Paul. He knew experientially the secret of the exchanged life–the self-life for the Christ-life. *'I am crucified... Christ lives in me...'* (Galatians 2:20). Prolonged physical life for Paul would simply mean that Christ

---

[28] Gordon Fee D., *Philippians*, InterVarsity, 70, 71, 1999

would continue to live in Paul to the benefit of the Philippians and others.[29]

Paul could joyfully face the unexpected because his life was hidden in Christ and nothing could separate him from Christ. As he said,

> *No, in all these things we are more than conquerors through him who loved us. For I am convinced that neither death nor life, neither angels nor demons, neither the present nor the future, not any powers, neither height nor depth, nor anything else in all creation, will be able to separate us from the love of God that is in Christ Jesus our Lord* (Romans 8:37-39).

Expecting the Unexpected

What is it that constitutes an emergency when it comes to your health? Someone asked that question because researchers at Children's Hospital in Boston found that emergency room visits at hospitals in Boston slowed significantly when the Red Sox were in the baseball World Series in 2004. During especially crucial matchups, such as Game 7 of the league championship series and the final game of the World Series, emergency-room traffic fell by up to 20 percent, as fans stayed glued to their TV sets. "It's as if when they look at the TV and see what's happening, they say, 'My infected lung, it's not so bad,'" reported one emergency room physician. Researchers say that people apparently have a flexible idea of what constitutes an "emergency," especially if they're caught up in the excitement of a big game. "The heart attacks, the strokes, they will come in no matter what's

---

[29] Malone, 39, 40

going on," says this same physician. "That patient with pneumonia, the patient with an asthma attack will say, 'Maybe I can ride this out at home.'"[30]

It would seem that Paul had learned to be content as to the unexpected divine providence of God. No matter what happens, no matter how much of a surprise it is, Paul has learned to expect the unexpected from his Lord. The fact that he is in a Roman prison, was more than likely unexpected, but when it is in the plans of God, it is as if Paul was saying, "I can ride this out anywhere, because it is the Lord's will and He will empower me to get through it."

Motivational speaker Earl Nightingale once told the story of an American team of mountain climbers who set out to conquer Mount Everest. Before the team left the U.S. a psychiatrist interviewed them. Each was asked individually, privately, "Will you get to the top of Everest?" There was a wide assortment of answers. "Well, Doc, I'll do my best." "I'm sure going to try." Each knew how formidable the challenge was. But one of them, a slightly built team member, gave a totally different answer. When the psychiatrist asked him the question, he thought for a moment and then quietly answered. "Yes, I will." Not surprisingly, he was the first to make it to the peak of Mt. Everest.

Nightingale comments:

> Yes, I will–three of the most potent words in our language. Whether spoken quietly, loudly, or silently, those three words have propelled more people to success and have been responsible for more human achievement than all other words in the English language combined.[31]

---

[30] Dynamic Preaching, January 2005
[31] Dan Mangler, Sunday_Sermons, January, 2005

Joyfully Facing the Unexpected

This story reminds us of another man who said, "Yes, I will," and he said it with the faith of a child of God, not with a false hope in the achievement of man. Paul is that man, and he said, *"What shall I do Lord"* (Acts 22:10)? He understood that all of his plans and achievements before that moment in time had been accomplished by man's ability, and they were nothing but rubbish, compared to the knowledge of Jesus Christ (3:7-9).

Paul knew that our God is a God of surprises. He also knew that whatever the reason God had for him to be in a Roman prison, that it was to better fulfill His plan for the furtherance of the gospel. We do not want to worship a God who is always predictable. We are reminded daily that our God sees the whole picture of mankind's dilemma and can rescue those who seek Him no matter whether the plan is within our reasoning ability or not. Thus, we understand Paul's challenge to us; *"Rejoice, again I say rejoice."*

Questions for Review

1. What is the purpose of the Excedrin Resource Center?
2. What does the title, *Joyfully Facing the Unexpected* mean?
3. How do we know that Paul was chained?
4. What was Paul's motive for preaching the gospel?
5. What did Paul say was the motive for preaching by his enemies?
6. What was Cloud and Townsend's conclusion on the concept of happiness?
7. What did Kushner's book site as a reason for God's not saving His Son?
8. What was Yancey's response to Kushner?

Lesson Four
(Chapter 1:27-30)

Joyfully Contending for the Faith

Whatever happens, conduct yourselves in a manner worthy of the gospel of Christ. Then, whether I come and see you or only hear about you in my absence, I will know that you stand firm in one spirit, contending as one man for the faith of the gospel without being frightened in any way by those who oppose you. This is a sign to them that they will be destroyed, but that you will be saved–and that by God. For it has been granted to you on behalf of Christ not only to believe on him, but also to suffer for him, since you are going through the same struggle you saw I had, and now hear that I still have.

Mark Twain was a writer of great charm and wit. Twain could communicate important insights in a way that won him many admirers. He was welcome in the highest social and literary circles both in this country and abroad. On one of his trips abroad the Emperor of Germany sent an invitation for him to come to the palace to dine with the royal family. When Twain's little daughter heard about it, she exclaimed, "Daddy, you know most everybody in the whole world now, don't you…except God?" Out of the mouths of babes![32]

The apostle Paul tells us that we must stand for the truth of

---

[32] Dynamic Preaching, July 2004

the Word of God, and prove all things in accordance with it being recognized as the absolute authority of God. Paul says,

> *For you were once darkness, but now you are light in the Lord. Live as children of light (for the fruit of the light consists in all goodness, righteousness and truth) and find out what pleases the Lord. Have nothing to do with the fruitless deeds of darkness, but rather expose them* (Ephesians 5:8-11).

In our society, the idea of there being such a thing as an absolute truth is foreign to the non-believer. In fact, many people in our world today believe that they are the final arbiter of truth. It is only how they feel that has any relevancy to truth. It is common to hear that, "what is truth to one person may not be truth to another." Therefore, there is not a belief in absolute truth in the minds of many in our culture today; only the opinions of each as they apply to their own lives. Situationalism has captured the hearts of many in our society today. This is the belief that it is the situation one finds himself in and the choice that works best in accordance with one's opinion of how the situation affects him/her that becomes the final authority.

For the true believer, the thought of the Bible as being anything other than "word for word" inspired of God, is an unrealistic concept. As Christians, we must contend for the *faith* in light of the fact that it is a part of our calling. Paul said,

> *All Scripture is God-breathed and is useful for teaching, rebuking, correcting, and training in righteousness, so that the man of God may be thoroughly equipped for every good work* (2 Timothy 3:16, 17).

Charlie Reese, syndicated columnist, illustrated the results of this non-judgmentalism in our society as follows:

> Somebody said every civilization is only a generation away from barbarism. What throws the switch is when the older generations lose their courage and their will to defend the values of their civilization.
>
> One defends a value first of all by practicing it. One defends a value by holding up examples for public praise and–this is absolutely necessary–by condemning those who reject those values. One defends a value by being intolerant of those who oppose it!
>
> Today, too many Americans are afraid. They are afraid to defend even courtesy. They are afraid not to laugh at vulgarisms. They are afraid to defend their own cultural values. Some are even afraid to assert that they believe in anything at all. The supply of criminals will be endless until we find the will and the courage to civilize the little barbarians before they grow into big ones.[33]

It would seem to the casual observer today that the church is, in general, in the very state described by Mr. Reese. Have we not allowed ourselves to accept most of the progressive changes in our faith that are contrary to the will of God? Are we standing for the truth of God's Word and the design of the New Testament Church? Are we losing the respect for an absolute authority in our Christian walk?

---

[33] Strengthening the Focus Magazine, January 1998

Columnist Cal Thomas, a believer, recounts the following story from a lecture given at the University of Michigan:

> The young woman tentatively approached the microphone to ask a question following my lecture at the University of Michigan. She said she disagreed with much of what I said, especially my contention that our nation needs to promote values rooted in certain fixed absolutes in order to repair a society that is increasingly dysfunctional and socially chaotic.
>
> I asked her, 'If you don't like my value system, what would you recommend to replace it?' She said she was not sure. 'What year are you in and what is your major?' I asked. 'I'm a senior and my major is ethics,' she said. 'On what do you base your own ethics?' I queried. 'I don't know,' she replied. 'I'm still trying to work that out.' Nearly 16 years of schooling at a cost of tens of thousands of dollars have left this student and many like her unable to think. It isn't entirely her fault. She is the victim of a failed public education system that has so 'dumbed down' a generation of young people that they think 'wisdom' refers to their teeth.[34]

In reference to our public school systems Dr. Brad Harrab, editor of Think Magazine, states:

> As the 'No Child Left Behind' era was ushered in, it seemed like our common sense in this country was ushered out. Children are no longer encouraged to think critically, reflect, or discuss but rather they are

---

[34] Ibid,

expected to master the art of memorization in order to become expert test takers. We have produced at least one generation (probably two) of standardized test takers. If we are honest with ourselves, we admit that our children are mastering the art of regurgitation factoids.[35]

Dr. Harrab emphasizes the fact that Christian parents need to investigate Home Schooling. In his lectures across the country, he points out the value of Home Schooling with a Christian curriculum that allows the parents to have control of the material the children are learning from and the fact that parents can teach Bible and lessons on character building. He also emphasizes the fact that our public schools are so infiltrated with teaching evolution and subjects of moral character that support various positions Christians cannot embrace. The point is that public schools do not strengthen the character of the students to endure hardships and make good choices with moral issues.

As we live in this society, we must understand the fact that the Bible is being reduced to a history book that has no real authority, and a dominate theory is that man is his own authority. If we do not know the truth of Scripture, and don't stand for it, who will, and what does such a position say about our faith?

The Fear Factor

Avon Malone in his wonderful little commentary on Philippians titled, *Press to the Prize*, makes this statement in reference to Paul's admonishing the Philippian church to not be frightened:

---

[35] Brad Harrab, *The Public School System is a Failed Model*, Think Magazine, July 2011

Picture Philippi in Paul's day proud of itself as a little Rome and suspicious of persons and movements not aligned with Rome and loyal to Caesar. Quite possibly there was an element of anti-Semitic bias in Philippi (Acts 16:20, 21). It was the kind of place that could make it difficult for real disciples of the Christ. Paul makes explicit references to their adversaries indicating that their opposition was sufficiently intense to cause terror (v. 28). Their opponents must not be allowed to frighten (*stampede*, as with livestock) them. Their conflict Paul describes with a word for the gladiatorial contests. Though the opposition is intense and the struggle severe, Paul calls for courage. Dauntlessness, bravery, courage under fire is that for which Paul pleads.[36]

All of us experience fear in our lives from time to time. The kind of fear Paul is talking about and the Bible condemns, is allowing fear to control the disciple when in danger of persecution or death (Revelation 21:8). It is a fact that the fear of man is the reason for many a disciple to forsake the faith or to avoid letting people know who they are. But Jesus says,

> *Do not be afraid of those who kill the body but cannot kill the soul. Rather, be afraid of the One who can destroy both soul and body in hell* (Matthew 10:28).

---

[36] Malone 47

Dr. James Dobson, a well known psychologist, revealed one time in his Focus on the Family Magazine,

> . . . that he saw a fascinating television documentary on the subject of elephants and their behavioral characteristics. The program was videotaped in India, where the magnificent pachyderms are trained to serve their human masters. Of course, if elephants knew how strong they were they would never yield to the domination of anything, but they are subjected to a stressful form of 'brainwashing,' which takes the fight out of them. The process begins with three days of total isolation from man or beast. Female elephants and their young are remarkably social animals, and they react to loneliness in the same way humans do. They grieve and fret and long for their peers. At that precise moment of vulnerability, they are brought to a nighttime ceremony of fire. Then for many hours in the flickering light, they are screamed at, intimidated, stroked and ordered back and forth. By morning, half crazed, the elephants have yielded. Their wills have been broken. Man is the master.

Dr. Dobson continues:

Even though I understand the economic need for working elephants in India, there is still something sad about their plight. These wonderfully intelligent animals are transformed from freedom to slavery in a single evening. Their fragile emotions are manipulated to destroy their independence and curb their individuality. Somehow, I wish it weren't true.

Dr. Dobson then compares this scene with childhood when he says,

> Then as I watched the documentary, I was struck by the parallel between these elephants and us fragile human beings. We too are social creatures, born with irrepressible needs to be loved and accepted by our parents and peers. In fact, to deprive us of this emotional support during early childhood is to risk crippling us for life.[37]

Our world is not conditioned to build Christian character and faith in the Supreme Being. Because of sin, and a rejection of the Bible, our world is prone to self-destruction and degradation, and Paul confirms such a conclusion (Romans 1:18-32). The distinction between Christians living by faith and a secular world is getting more pronounced every day. The difference is because of allowing immorality to reign in our culture.

Among those murdered in the Columbine High School shootings, on April 20, 1999, was a young Christian student named Rachel Scott. At her funeral service, Rachel's minister read an excerpt from the girl's diary detailing the sacrifices she made when she became a Christian. "I lost all of my friends," she wrote. "Now that I have begun to 'walk my talk,'" she continued, "they make fun of me." Rachel goes on to tell of how her former friends gossiped about her and called her names because of her faith in Christ. But she ends this entry by writing, "I am not going to apologize for speaking the name of Christ... If my friends have to become my enemies for me to be with my best friend, Jesus, then that's fine with me."

It has been reported that when the gun toting boy asked

---

[37] James Dobson, Focus on the Family Magazine, May 1986

of the students who was a Christian, Rachel acknowledged that she was, and was then shot to death.[38] When you are a high school student, losing your friends can truly be a source of suffering. In some cases, of course, it can also be the best thing that ever happened to you.

This story perhaps can give us a better understanding of what the inspired prophets and apostles mean when they tell us to face trials and tribulations with JOY in our hearts. Again Paul encourages us to *"Rejoice in the Lord always, I will say it again; Rejoice!"* (4:4).

LaGard Smith, in his provocative book, *When Choice Becomes God*, makes these comments about our culture,

> We are now engaged in a great civil war, testing whether that nation, or any nation, so conceived and so dedicated, can long endure. We are yet on a great battlefield of that war.
>
> With those words Abraham Lincoln not only dedicated the cemetery at Gettysburg, but captured the nobility of the great national struggle over slavery which threatened to divide the nation. Never in the intervening century have we faced so grave a moral crisis as the one about which we in our generation have become deeply divided: the battle over abortion. Yet our current civil war is not specifically about abortion at least not in the long run.

Smith goes on to say,

> And at the core of the revolution is *choice*: The right for us to decide for ourselves, and the right of others

---

[38] Dynamic Preaching, May 2000

to decide for themselves. Being nonjudgmental about others seems to be our only guarantee of their being nonjudgmental about us. In order to maintain our own right of choice, we have become willing to honor all the choices of others: hence, the language of a pro-choice generation.[39]

The Validity of a Sign

One commentator says of chapter one verse 28;

Paul says that this circumstance of persecution, if they evinced such a spirit as he wished, would be to them an evidence of two things: 1) of the destruction of those who were engaged in the persecution. This would be, because they knew that such persecutors could not ultimately prevail. Persecution of the church would be a certain indication that they who did it would be finally destroyed. 2) It would be a proof of their own salvation, because it would show that they were the friends of the Redeemer; and they had the assurance that all those who were persecuted for his sake would be saved.[40]

Paul seems to suggest that the very fact of the Philippian church undergoing persecution reflects God's judgment on the persecutors, even if they cannot see the sign. It is interesting that the contrast between Christian disciples and the world is more evident because of persecution and that God has granted the privilege to his followers to suffer for the

---

[39] LaGard Smith, *When Choice Becomes God*, 9-10
[40] Barnes Notes on Philippians

cause of Christ. In other words, Christians can be confident of two facts as they face persecution: 1) facing persecution is a sign of the faithfulness of the Christian, and 2) if the Christian is not controlled by fear, and he stands for the truth, it is a sign of God's condemnation of the persecutors. Paul is trying to encourage the church of Philippi to endure the suffering they are going through, because it is a sign of God's plan for the faithful to know of their salvation. God does comfort us. Paul says,

> *Praise be to the God and Father of our Lord Jesus Christ, the Father of compassion and the God of all comfort, who comforts us in all our troubles, so that we can comfort those in any trouble with the comfort we ourselves have received from God* (2 Corinthians 1:3, 4).

A reporter tells of standing in the yard of Amelia Earhart's old home up in Atchison, Kansas. As he looked far down the bluff at the Missouri River, he thought of this Kansas girl who would learn to fly. She was the first woman to fly across the Atlantic, first woman to fly from Hawaii to California, first woman to attempt an around the world solo flight. Last heard from in 1937 far out over the Pacific, her last words were simple: "Position doubtful." And then she was gone.[41]

There are many people in our world that can identify with those words: "Position doubtful." "Where is God when we need Him," we ask when we face trials and temptations. There are many people in society who can't see the signs that reflect a world that is lost and can't find its way. Paul is telling the Philippian church, and all Christians everywhere,

---

[41] Dynamic Preaching, June 1998

that their *position is secure* when they face persecution for the cause of Christ, because it is a sign of faithfulness to God, and He will not forget it, and He will continue to strengthen the faithful in their trials as they stand for truth. This is the motivation behind Paul's joy in contending for the faith.

Purpose is Powerful

People cannot live without meaning. Where there is no meaning there is no power. We don't have to look very far to see this phenomenon at work. Charles Colson writes,

> During World War II, a group imprisoned at a Nazi concentration camp in Hungary converted waste products into synthetic alcohol to be used as a fuel additive. One day the Allies bombed the camp and almost destroyed the building where the alcohol was manufactured. The next morning, the guards decided to punish the inmates. They forced them to take all the rubble from the air-raid and arrange it at one end of a field. When the prisoners finished this task, the guards ordered them to carry it back to the other end. This went on, back and forth, for several weeks until the prisoners began to break under the strain. Some tried to escape and were killed. Others electrocuted themselves by jumping on the high-voltage fence that surrounded the camp. A few lost their minds because the work made no sense their lives had no meaning.[42]

We must have meaning in life. We must have a reason for being. Where there is no purpose there is no power. Paul

---

[42] Charles Colson, *Kingdoms in Conflict*

is telling the Philippian church and all who claim to be disciples of Christ that God grants us the power to suffer for God's cause, and that there is power in such suffering.

In a 1995 report on 232 people who underwent elective open-heart surgery, it was found that those who received no strength or comfort from religion were more likely to die within six months of the operation.[43]

A decade-long study of 2,700 people showed that after accounting for all risk factors, only one social attribute–increased church attendance–lowered mortality rates. Among women recovering from hip fractures, those with stronger religious beliefs and practices were less depressed and could walk further when they were discharged. In a rigorously controlled study of elderly women, the less religious had mortality levels twice that of the faithful. A review of one group of 200 studies, suggest that religion has positive effects on diseases ranging from cervical cancer to stroke.[44]

Standing for the truth of God's Word gives us meaning and purpose in life. It convicts believers of the reason for living that God has given us. When Paul says that God has granted us the privilege of suffering for the cause of Christ, he is stating a truth that suffering for a noble purpose creates in us a power that transcends any other force in this world. Therefore, we can JOYFULLY contend for the faith, knowing the power it gives us to face life.

---

[43] Psychology Today, July 1995
[44] Ibid.

Questions for Review

1. How does suffering give us power in life?
2. What was the Fear Factor referred to in the book?
3. What was Cal Thomas' point?
4. What was Dr. Harrab's conclusion on our public school system?
5. What was the point in regards to The Validity of a Sign?
6. Who was the girl shot at Columbine High School?
7. Why was she killed?
8. Why is Purpose Powerful?

Lesson Five
(Chapter 2:1-11)

Joyfully Possessing the Mind of Christ

If you have any encouragement from being united with Christ, if any comfort from his love, if any fellowship with the Spirit, if any tenderness and compassion, then make my joy complete by being like-minded, having the same love, being one in spirit and purpose. Do nothing out of selfish ambition or vain conceit, but in humility consider others better than yourselves. Each of you should look not only to your own interests, but also to the interests of others.

Your attitude should be the same as that of Christ Jesus: Who, being in very nature God, did not consider equality with God something to be grasped, but made himself nothing, taking the very nature of a servant, being made in human likeness. And being found in appearance as a man, he humbled himself and became obedient to death even death on a cross! Therefore God exalted him to the highest place and gave him the name that is above every name, that at the name of Jesus every knee should bow, in heaven and on earth and under the earth, and every tongue confess that Jesus Christ is Lord, to the glory of God the Father.

There are many diverse philosophies in the world today, some of them quite bizarre. The September 5, 2005, issue of *Newsweek* magazine focused on "Spirituality in America." The author of the lead article makes the point that more and more people today are creating their own religions out of a mix of orthodox and non-traditional practices and beliefs. Among the many people quoted in the central article was a young woman, a student getting her doctorate in Religion and Nature at the University of Florida. The article's author noted that this young woman's idea of worship consists of "composting, recycling, and daily five-mile runs."[45]

What a contrast between a self-serving so-called religion and the true religion of the Son of God who sacrificed Himself for us all. This section of Philippians is about the *submissive mind*. Paul's discussion on the incarnation and ultimate victory of Christ is a beautiful description of what it means to be submissive to the Father. It is of course a misunderstood passage by many and has often been interpreted as a description of how Christ gave up His deity when He became flesh.

Jackson writes,

> Paul affirms that Christ is *existing* in the form of God. 'Existing' is a present tense participle derived from [Greek word] *huparchon*. It denotes to be, to be in existence, involving an existence or condition both previous to the circumstances mentioned in the context, and continuing after it. Here, it carries with it the two facts of the antecedent Godhood of Christ, previous to His Incarnation, and the continuance of His Godhead at and after the event of His birth.[46]

---

[45] Jerry Adler, *In Search of the Spiritual*, Newsweek, August 29, 2005
[46] Jackson, 74

The point to be made here is that Christ's submission to the will of God was not in the giving up of His deity, but in the changing of His role. Jackson again clarifies it by saying,

> If, though, Christ possessed an equality with the Father, how does one explain such passages as John 14:28, 'The Father is greater than I'; this verse, and a few others of similar nature (cf. 1 Corinthians 11:3), refer to that phase of the Lord's existence *after* He emptied Himself of His equality with the Father, i.e., in His incarnate state. The emptying involved a change in *roles*, but not a divesting of the divine nature.[47]

False Religion

In the Book of Joel, chapter 2, the prophet Joel is speaking to the people of Israel, but he could just as easily be speaking to us today. He is in despair over how the people are practicing an empty form of religion without any heartfelt commitment to God. They observe all the necessary rituals, says Joel, but their hearts are far from God. Their faith makes no difference in their lives. Their sins have separated them from the Lord, and have made them a symbol of hypocrisy among their neighbors.

The pagan people who live all around them have heard of the God of Israel the Lord God Jehovah, the one true God. They hear that this is the Creator God, the Sovereign Ruler over the Universe. And yet, the pagans can't help but notice that the people who supposedly serve this exalted God are living empty and sometimes even wicked lives. They are no different from everybody else. Their lives lack any higher

---

[47] Jackson, 75, 76

purpose, and their faith lacks any redemptive power. And so the prophet Joel urges the people to repent, to return to the promises, purposes, and power of the Lord.

In Joel 2 the Lord says,

Even now, declares the Lord, return to me with all your heart, with fasting and weeping and mourning. Rend your heart and not your garments. Return to the Lord your God, for he is gracious and compassionate, slow to anger and abounding in love, and he relents from sending calamity ...Blow the trumpet in Zion... bring together the elders, gather the children, those nursing at the breast. Let the bridegroom leave his room and the bride her chamber. Let the priests, who minister before the Lord, weep between the temple porch and the altar. Let them say, 'Spare your people, O Lord. Do not make your inheritance an object of scorn, a byword among the nations. Why should they say among the peoples, 'Where is their God?' (Joel 2:12-17).

Vance Havner, a prominent author and preacher, made a statement in reference to this passage from Joel 2. Havner believed this message hits too close to home for most modern churches. As he said,

There ought to be enough divine electricity in every church to give everybody in the congregation either a charge or a shock! What do you mean by singing *Onward Christian Soldiers*, when most of your army has deserted? I agree with Joel, says Havner.

I'm embarrassed when pagans walk by our empty churches, look in on our feeble ceremonies; see us swapping members from church to church, moving corpses from one mortician to another, preaching a dynamite gospel and living firecracker lives.[48]

It is evident in Paul's statement that there will come a time when all will bow down to Jesus Christ and call Him Lord, whether or not they believe in Him. We are able to make our choices today, whether we want to have a frivolous religion with a theology of self-exultation or self-sacrifice, but the time will come when all will acknowledge Jesus as Lord even if they don't want to at this time.

> The day will come when people will call Jesus Lord, but they will do so to the glory of God the Father. The whole aim of Jesus is not his own glory but God's. Paul is clear about the only and ultimate supremacy of God. In the first letter to the Corinthians, he writes that in the end the Son himself shall be subject to the one who put all things in subjection under him (1 Corinthians 15:28). Jesus draws men and women to himself that he may draw them to God. In the Philippian church, there were some whose aim was to gratify a selfish ambition; the aim of Jesus was to serve others, no matter what depths of self-renunciation that service might involve. In the Philippian church, there were those whose aim was to focus people's eyes upon themselves; the aim of Jesus was to focus people's eyes upon God.[49]

We have many false religions in force today, which all claim enlightenment. Phil Sanders, a good friend and

---

[48] Dynamic Preaching, April 2001
[49] Barclay, 47

speaker of *In Search of the Lord's Way*, a national Television program, states:

> A longstanding debate has existed between postmodern progressives and conservatives as to whether Enlightenment thinkers such as John Locke (1632-1704) and the inductive reasoning of the rationalists brought about restoration hermeneutics or whether the hermeneutics arose from Scripture itself. But critics who wish to make New Testament Christianity the product of the Enlightenment and to make truth the product of modern rationalism actually reveal their own myopic biases. They want to impose their perception on to the truth. They are shortsighted, forgetting God's message in Christ arose in the first century. For them to allow culture to rise above Christ, they must make what is eternal into what is temporal.[50]

The Submissive Mind

God has always emphasized the value of a submissive mind. The story of the Pharisee and the tax collector surely confirms His feelings about pride, and how we must rid ourselves of this attitude in our lives (Luke 18:9-14). Subjection does not mean the same as inferiority. All of us are in subjection to someone, whether it is our employer, boss, government, police, etc.; in all of these cases, being in subjection does not mean that we are necessarily inferior to the person or persons to whom we are in subjection. Paul begins chapter two by encouraging the church at Philippi to submit to one another.

---

[50] Phil Sanders, *A Faith Built on Sand*, Gospel Advocate, 36

Paul knew that 'only the lowly minded can be like-minded.' The apostle knew that some motives are potentially divisive. Therefore, he urged 'doing nothing through faction or through vain glory.' Human pride can be explosive. Egocentricity and a partisan spirit are the enemies of authentic unity. Therefore, Paul pleads for lowliness of mind.[51]

A very similar appeal appears in another of Paul's prison letters:

As a prisoner for the Lord, then, I urge you to live a life worthy of the calling you have received. Be completely humble and gentle; be patient, bearing with one another in love. Make every effort to keep the unity of the Spirit through the bond of peace. There is one body and one Spirit–just as you were called–one Lord, one faith, one baptism; one God and Father of all, who is over all and through all and in all (Ephesians 4:1-6).

In the Book of James, James says that God is a jealous God as well as a gracious God. He says, "*But he gives us more grace. That is why Scripture says: God opposes the proud but gives grace to the humble*" (James. 4:6). We already know that God's ideal is total commitment. But all of us would have to admit that there have been times when we have forsaken the Lord to go after what we want. The Lord makes great demands and gives great grace to fulfill them (Proverbs 3:34; 1 Peter 4:10).

The choice is obvious for believers. We can humble ourselves and receive God's grace or continue in our self-

---

[51] Malone, 50

serving attitude and experience God's resistance. It is pride that often causes us to misapply Scripture and to interpret it in a way that conforms to our lifestyle and desire for power.

James tells us to rid our lives of selfishness and develop a relationship with God. In order to rid our lives of selfishness and let God be in control, James tells Christians to not give in to their desires but to *"Submit yourselves, then, to God. Resist the devil, and he will flee from you"* (James 4:7). The word *submit* is primarily a military term and means, *to stand in rank*. To be cured of selfishness, a Christian must place himself under orders of the Lord.

The important part of this submission is to decide whose side we are on. James not only says that you must *"Submit yourselves therefore to God,"* he also says, *"Resist the devil and he will flee from you."* The word *resist* is not a passive word. It refers to *active* opposition. It is another military term that literally means, "To set in battle array against." The picture is of the Christian soldier in his place in the army of God, fighting with all his might against the forces of evil (Ephesians 6:10-18). If you do actively oppose the devil, he will flee from you. Our enemy is formidable, but not irresistible. The devil has no power over the Christian other than the ability to make evil look attractive. Once we get by the glitter and resist the devil's allurements, we are promised that he will run from us.

James goes on to say, *"Humble yourselves before the Lord, and he will lift you up"* (James 4:10). Being submissive to God, leads to great spiritual blessings. The exaltation about which James is writing is to a higher life.

> The picture James portrayed was a person falling prostrate before an oriental monarch, begging for mercy. The monarch leans from the throne and lifts the petitioner's face from the ground. The person rises

with great joy, knowing the king has granted his request.[52]

Metacognition

Metacognition is the ability to think about thinking to understand and control one's thought processes. As counselees progress in therapy, they become adept at metacognition; recognizing inflexible and destructive thoughts and replacing them with adaptive ones. In psychology, this type of methodology is called Cognitive Therapy.

In Cognitive Therapy, counselors have traditionally required skills of metacognition. Those looking for spiritual help are often directed to passages of Scripture that require metacognition. This common methodology provides a sense of safety for many Christians as they begin Cognitive Therapy–safety that promotes a healing, therapeutic atmosphere. Consider the following example of familiar Scripture passages emphasizing metacognition:

Do not conform any longer to the pattern of this world, but be transformed by the renewing of your mind. Then you will be able to test and approve, what God's will is–his good, pleasing and perfect will (Romans 12:2).

The idea of renewing our minds requires us to understand our thoughts and feelings and examine them critically in the light of Scripture and Christian theology. The context of this passage suggests it is our Christian obligation, and act of

---

[52] Bill Hooten, John Justin, Ken Wilson, *Faith That Makes A Difference*, Agape Publishing, 129

worship, to renew our minds. As a result, many Christians are experienced in the art of introspection due to the requirements of becoming a Christian and growing in the faith (see also Ephesians 4:20-24). Some are skilled at analyzing their thoughts and looking for alternative ways of thinking, while others introspect but come to inflexible or unreasonable conclusions.

Another passage we need to consider is:

We demolish arguments and every pretension that sets itself up against the knowledge of God, and we take captive every thought to make it obedient to Christ (2 Corinthians 10:5).

In the context of waging a war against the standards of the world, the apostle Paul clearly emphasizes thinking about thinking (see also Philippians 4:8). He admonishes his readers to think like Christ thinks, seeking pure, truthful thoughts. Metacognition helps make the same connection between thoughts and feelings. Dysfunctional, inflexible thinking leads to negative feelings, while accurate, true thinking leads to peace.

Thus, accurate, critical, flexible thinking is the key to changing unwanted feelings. Therefore, the concept of metacognition works well for Christians who want to emphasize *truth seeking* above *happiness seeking*, because teaching critical thinking skills is an essential part of possessing the mind of Christ.

It is evident that in the Bible there were godly men and women who altered their beliefs and obeyed, sometimes sacrificing happiness to do so. Throughout the Scriptures, God's people stood firm in the midst of tribulation because they were committed to godliness through truthful and productive thinking. The following are examples of such:

- Abraham chose to believe God's promise of a child though it seemed impossible.
- Job survived crisis after crisis and resisted his wife's and friend's conclusions that his troubles were caused by his sin.
- Daniel obediently prayed, though he knew he could be punished with death in the lion's den.
- David thought of God's power rather than Goliath's size.
- Hosea chose to forgive Gomer's unfaithfulness, overcoming his anger.
- The apostle Paul sought obedience above personal safety.

These examples demonstrate independent, critical thinking in the midst of danger or emotional pain. It is useful in thinking about thinking to speculate on the thought processes that were involved and how *truth thinking* won out over *happiness thinking*.

Thinking that Saves

Paul was facing his problems with the people at Rome as well as with people in Philippi, and it was the latter that concerned him the most. Paul wanted them to see that the basic cause was selfishness, and the cause of selfishness is pride (Romans 12:3).

The *mind of Christ* means the *attitude* Christ exhibited. After all, "outlook determines outcome." If the outlook is selfish, the actions will be divisive and destructive. Christ did not consider His equality with God as something selfishly to be held unto. He did not think of Himself, He thought of others. It is like a LOOSE WIRE, attached to nothing and creating nothing; but when it surrenders to a dynamo, it throbs with energy, with light and power. It lives by living for something beyond itself. Jesus said, *"For whoever wants to save his life will lose it, but whoever loses his life for me will find it"* (Matthew 16:25).

No one has the right to demand his or her will over the church. Jesus did not pretend to be a servant; He was not an actor playing a role. He emptied himself! Meaning He laid aside His privileges. This is the essence of the *submissive mind*. *"Just as the Son of Man did not come to be served, but to serve, and to give His life as a ransom for many"* (Matthew 20:28). Self-surrender delivers us from the fear of what other people think of us and frees us to serve others.

Many people are willing to serve others if it does not cost anything, but if there is a price to pay, they suddenly lose interest. "Ministry that costs nothing accomplishes nothing." (J. H. Jowett) The person with the submissive mind does not avoid sacrifice. He lives for the glory of God and the good of others, and if paying the price will honor Christ and help others, he/she will do it. This is the difference with those who are programmed and caught up in HAPPINESS SEEKING and those who have learned to sacrifice and live a life of TRUTH SEEKING!

The paradox of the Christian life is that JOY comes from sacrifice and suffering. Paul says, *"In fact, everyone who wants to live a godly life in Christ Jesus will be persecuted"* (2 Timothy 3:12). We can't escape suffering for the cause of Christ, so it is evident that making happiness seeking a priority in our life will hinder us from being true disciples of Jesus.

A Christian sect in Japan called the "No-self Sect," stated that they were denying self-will, by letting icy water flow over them in the dead of winter. The contradiction is that they usually sought an audience for the promoting of the exercise.

The whole purpose of Christ's humiliation and exaltation is the glory of God. Such is the essence of the SUBMISSIVE MIND. The person with such a mind, as he lives for others, must expect sacrifice and service. People cannot rob us of our JOY if we possess such a mind. Thinking of others as we serve the Lord, guarantees that we will experience the joy Paul proclaims. Therefore, we can REJOICE as we work towards possessing the mind of Christ.

Questions for Review

1. What is the basis for possessing the mind of Christ?
2. How does Thinking Save?
3. What was the point the prophet Joel was making in Joel chapter 2?
4. What did Christ give up when he became the Son of Man?
5. What does it mean to have the Submissive Mind?
6. How would you define the term Metacognition?
7. What does the Mind of Christ mean?
8. What does James mean when he says, "Resist the Devil and he will flee from you?"

Lesson Six
(Chapter 2:12-18)

Joyfully Shining as the Stars in Heaven

Therefore, my dear friends, as you have always obeyed not only in my presence, but now much more in my absence continue to work out your salvation with fear and trembling, for it is God who works in you to will and to act according to his good purpose.

Do everything without complaining or arguing, so that you may become blameless and pure, children of God without fault in a crooked and depraved generation, in which you shine like stars in the universe as you hold out the word of life in order that I may boast on the day of Christ that I did not run or labor for nothing. But even if I am being poured out like a drink offering on the sacrifice and service coming from your faith, I am glad and rejoice with all of you. So you too should be glad and rejoice with me.

Danny Cox, a former Air Force pilot, who helped pioneer supersonic flights, reports,

There was a problem in the early jets with the process of ejecting pilots out of their seats. Ideally, the process went something like this: pull up both arm rests in the flight seat, squeeze the ejection triggers, let go of the flight seat and trigger the parachute. But some pilots made the mistake of holding onto the flight seat after ejecting from the plane. As long as they were still in the seat, their parachutes wouldn't open. Letting go of the seat meant letting go of anything solid and secure; it also meant survival. Holding on to the flight seat may have felt secure, but it resulted in a crash landing and certain death. Government engineers solved this problem by modifying the flight seat so that when the ejection trigger was pushed, the pilot's body was automatically forced out of the seat.[53]

In this section of Philippians, Paul is encouraging all Christians to work out your own salvation. It is an imperative statement to the effect that God expects us to be ready to work at changing our lifestyle behavior. It means that we must be ready to trade guilty pleasure for lasting joy. Some must be ready to reject comfort found in a bottle, or a sinful life; for the comfort that only a clear conscience and an authentic awareness of God's presence can bring. Sometimes you have to let go of something you once prized in order to take hold of that which is without price or priceless.

Psychologists like to talk about living a *self-actualized* life. Self-actualization is a term popularized by the psychologist Abraham Maslow years ago. Self-actualization lacks the richness of the new birth to which Christ calls us, but there are some similarities. A self-actualized person is an emotionally healthy and well-balanced individual. He, or she, is able to give and receive love. The self-actualized person finds purpose and meaning in life. He is inner-directed and

---

[53] Danny Cox and John Hoover, *Seize The Day*, Career Press, 49

doesn't need the approval of others. He exhibits a healthy sense of self-control, but does not need to control others. These are just a few of the traits of a self-actualized person.

During his doctoral studies, psychologist Wayne Dyer took a class in which he and his fellow students studied the traits of self-actualized people. For the midterm exam, the professor asked only one question; an essay question. Listen to this question and pose your own answer:

> A self-actualized person arrives at a dinner party at which everyone is dressed in formal attire tuxes and beautiful gowns. He is wearing blue jeans, a T-shirt, sneakers, and a baseball cap. What does he do?

None of the students passed the exam. The professor was looking for one particular answer, an answer that can be expressed in three simple words, "He wouldn't notice." A self-actualized person wouldn't notice appearances. He or she is tuned in to more important things.[54]

The apostle Paul is not talking about creating the ability to work out our own salvation by using our own skills, talents and positive self-esteem. Self-actualization has its strong points personality wise, but it is not the single goal of the Christian. Our mission is to do our part to meet the conditions of salvation as God does his part.

Again, Jackson comments,

> So he encourages the brethren to 'continue working out' their salvation. This exhortation assumes human free agency in the carrying on the work of one's salvation. In view of this admonition, how could one

---

[54] Dynamic Preaching, February 2003

possibly assert that man is 'wholly passive' with reference to his salvation.[55]

Malone adds,

> The Philippians are to work out their salvation with *fear and trembling*. There is no tension between these exhortations and John's statement, 'perfect love casts our fear' (1 John 4:18). The term 'fear' is used in various senses in Scripture. Fear can mean 'terror, horror, dread.' Or 'fear' can mean 'awe, reverence, respect.' Perfect love casts out the former but not the latter.[56]

God is the POWER SOURCE that motivates the submissive mind to be productive in everyday living. How could mortal man ever hope to achieve what Jesus Christ achieved? Paul is setting before us the divine *pattern* for the submissive mind and the divine power to accomplish what God has commanded. We cultivate the *submissive mind* by responding to the divine provisions God makes available to us.

The phrase "work out your salvation" probably has specific reference to the special problems at Philippi. But the statement also applies to the individual Christian. We are not to be cheap imitations of other people. Paul says, *"Follow my example, as I follow the example of Christ"* (1 Corinthians 11:1). As we allow God to achieve this purpose in our lives, we become better examples to the world.

The same God, who used Moses' rod, Gideon's pitchers,

---

[55] Jackson, 83, also A. T. Robertson, *Word Pictures in the New Testament*, IV, 446
[56] Malone, 63

and David's sling, used Paul's chains. Little did the Romans realize that the chains affixed to Paul would release him instead of bind him (2 Timothy 2:9). To begin with, these chains gave Paul contact with the lost. He even converted some who were of Caesar's household (4:22). When you have the single mind, you look upon your circumstances as God given opportunities for the furthering of the gospel. Paul is REJOICING at what God is going to do rather than regretting what God did not do.

Overcoming an Argumentative Spirit

Paul reminds the Philippians of the damage an argumentative spirit can cause the church. There is no joy in a spirit that always seeks an argument to win for the purpose of self-gratification. Most people consider it crucial to defend their position, when they are criticized. They feel that they have to prove that the criticism is totally wrong, and that they have been sadly misunderstood. They feel that the response they made was correct and reasonable, and that the other person is a poor judge, who has no right to criticize anyway. So they argue and plead their case, or attack the critic, probably because of their fear of looking less authoritative or capable. What remains in the end is anger and strained relationships. Rarely do people handle criticism effectively or biblically.

The best defense is a good offense. You can disarm the critic by agreeing that his criticism might be right, and you will evaluate it. Agreeing with the critic disarms him, and opens up more dialogue. Paul says,

> *Don't have anything to do with foolish and stupid arguments, because you know they produce quarrels. And the Lord's servant must not quarrel; instead, he*

must be kind to everyone, able to teach, not resentful. Those who oppose him he must gently instruct, in the hope that God will grant them repentance leading them to a knowledge of the truth, and that they will come to their senses and escape from the trap of the devil, who has taken them captive to do his will (2 Timothy 2:23-26).

When we have the presupposition that the critic is wrong, that we have been terribly misunderstood, we then tell ourselves that we will not survive another minute, unless we set things right, or prove the critic wrong. None of these common views are true. Strange as it may seem, much of the criticism is usually correct. Not always, but often. Not entirely correct, but correct enough in a large measure. Occasionally, of course, the critic is totally wrong.

Not only is criticism frequently correct, it may even be good for us, even though it may not feel good at the time. God can use criticism, even painful, unfair criticism, to call our attention to our need for change. Since God is at work to make us holy, we must not overlook the means He may choose to accomplish this work in us (Hebrews 12:7-11). It would seem that this is what Paul is talking about when he says that it is God who is at work in us. If any effort to improve relationships by communication is to succeed, the persons involved must learn to *listen*. *"If one listens to you, you have won your brother over,"* is how Jesus put it (Matthew 18:15). If Jesus' instructions to, *go and show him his fault*, is ignored, the importance He placed on listening is equally ignored. Undoubtedly, Paul is referencing the two sisters who are arguing in the congregation at Philippi, and trying to tell them that such behavior is of the world and is blameworthy (4:2, 3).

We must learn the skill of listening before we can

communicate well. No matter how well we may talk, without listening, our efforts will be in vain. We are responsible to develop our own listening skills, not someone else's. We must become the best communicator that we can be, because the welfare of our relationships and the example we provide to the world depends on it (James. 1:19). Paul stated it this way when he said,

> *Do not let any unwholesome talk come out of your mouths, but only what is helpful for building others up according to their needs, that it may benefit those who listen* (Ephesians 4:29).

"Me and My Narrowing Circle"

The following story by an unknown author reflects the damage that a judgmental and critical heart can create:

When I became a Christian, I drew a *very large circle* which included all who, like myself, had believed and had been baptized. I was happy in the thought that my brethren were many. But I soon learned to my sorrow that all my brethren were not true brethren. A man with a keen mind will learn a lot through observation, and I have been a close and constant observer of the brethren down through the years. In watching them, I have discovered their errors.

I drew *another circle*. Thereafter, I was forced, time and time again, to make *my circle* smaller so as to exclude the 'errorist,' for I could not, with good conscience, tolerate any people within *my circle* except those who, like myself, were right in all points of doctrine and practice. Every time I drew *my circle*, which was becoming progressively smaller, I placed myself inside where I belonged. By watching the lives of those left within *my circle*, I learned that some had sinned and made mistakes. I was sorely grieved. What could I do about this? What else could a righteous man do than that which I had already done? Good men must avoid sinful men.

So, in righteous indignation, *my circle* I drew again leaving the publican and sinners without, and 'me' and the 'righteous' within. I observed that many were self-righteous, unforgiving; they thought that they were the only 'good people' in the world. I do not like people who think too highly of themselves and set all others at naught. So, as a matter of discipline, *my circle* I drew again, leaving the self-righteous without and 'me' and the 'humble' within.

I heard ugly rumors about this brother and that. Brethren should not allow ugly rumors to get started. Hopefully I would never have such rumors circulate about me. Now, should a man with a good reputation be associated with brethren in bad repute? Should he not guard his own good name? In order to save my good name, *my circle* I drew again; leaving the disreputable without, and 'me' and the 'reputable' within.

My circle had become small. Yet I continued to watch the mistakes in the lives of the brethren. I learned that some of them, though not out-and-out sinners, were worldly minded. I have a way of knowing what brethren are thinking about! The pleasures in which they participate were questionable. They should not participate in innocent pleasures. For instance, they should not drink coffee, but like me, drink tea. So, through a solemn sense of duty, *my circle*, I drew again; leaving the worldly-minded out, and the spiritual within.

Now only my family and I were left. I wanted my family on the inside, because I love my family every member of it. I have a good family. The members of my family were always right except when they disagreed with me. Finally, my family and I had a fuss. There were two sides to this fuss. I was on one side and my family on the other. My side was right, and when a man is right he should be steadfast. In all my experience in church troubles, I have never been a factious man. I have always been identified with the true church and never the faction. So, in courage and determination, *my circle* I drew again; leaving my factious family on the outside, and me and myself within!

Experiencing the Joy Patience Brings

It seems that Paul could recall his days when perhaps he was more judgmental in his approach to ministry. When he and Barnabas had a sharp disagreement over the inclusion of John Mark in their 2nd missionary journey, they split up and went their separate ways (Acts 15:36-41). Jackson concludes,

> The disagreement between Paul and Barnabas was so 'sharp' the two decided to split up. The Greek word for 'sharp contention' (disagreement; NIV) was sometimes used by the physicians to denote the 'height of a fever.' In a way, it was a very sad day

though good eventually came from it.[57]

The disagreement was very contentious and caused Paul and Barnabas to go their separate ways. Paul took Silas and Barnabas took Mark as their partners in missions. Later Paul will say to Timothy, during his second imprisonment and shortly before his death, *". . .Get Mark and bring him with you, because he is helpful to me in my ministry"* (2 Timothy 4:11). Is it at all possible that Paul was too harsh with Barnabas in his judgment of Mark? After all, Paul is a human being, highly motivated and intense in fulfilling his divine commission. Did he learn something about patience when he was in the Roman prison and penned the Philippian letter stating, *"... I have learned to be content whatever the circumstances"* (4:11)? Had he finally developed the patience so aptly displayed in Barnabas, when he patiently mentored Paul when no one else would have anything to do with him?

Paul could now say with conviction that true JOY comes from learning and experiencing contentment, and it is a process that even the fact of possessing miraculous power could not accelerate in him. Jackson also adds,

> The apostle says that 'in everything and in all things' (i.e., in all conditions of life) he has 'learned the secret' ('am instructed' KJV). The verb is *memuemai*, the perfect tense, passive voice form of *mueo*. The passive voice of the verb would suggest that the 'learning' or 'instruction' came from a source outside of Paul (namely the providential events that had shaped his ministry). The perfect tense [in the Greek]

---

[57] Wayne Jackson, *Acts—From Jerusalem to Rome,* Courier Publications, (2000) 191

stresses the abiding effect of these strengthening lessons in this great man's life.[58]

The joy that Paul felt, and so aptly expressed in the epistle to the Philippian church, was a natural by-product of learning to be content to a greater degree in the latter part of his life. It is such a powerful testimony of The Joy Principle in a Christian's life.

---

[58] Jackson, 152

Questions for Review

1. What is the meaning of "work out your salvation?"
2. How would you overcome an argumentative spirit?
3. What does patience have to do with joy?
4. What does Paul mean when he says we are to "Shine as the Stars in Heaven?"
5. How would you define the term "self-actualization?"
6. How would you define the concept "active listening?"
7. Did Paul behave properly in his sharp contention with Barnabas?
8. Should Paul have taken Mark with him regardless of Mark's weakness?

Lesson Seven
(Chapter 2:19-30)

Joyfully Serving as Christ's Disciple

I hope in the Lord Jesus to send Timothy to you soon, that I also may be cheered when I receive news about you. I have no one else like him, who takes a genuine interest in your welfare. For everyone looks out for his own interests, not those of Jesus Christ. But you know that Timothy has proved himself, because as a son with his father he has served with me in the work of the gospel. I hope, therefore, to send him as soon as I see how things go with me. And I am confident in the Lord that I myself will come soon.

But I think it is necessary to send back to you Epaphroditus, my brother, fellow worker and fellow soldier, who is also your messenger, whom you sent to take care of my needs. For he longs for all of you and is distressed because you heard he was ill. Indeed he was ill, and almost died. But God had mercy on him, and not on him only but also on me, to spare me sorrow upon sorrow. Therefore I am all the more eager to send him, so that when you see him again you may be glad and I may have less anxiety. Welcome him in the Lord with great joy, and honor men like him, because he almost died for the work of Christ, risking his life to make up for the help you could not give me.

In the 1988 Olympics, the world assumed that the United States would be victorious in the 400-meter relay. They simply were the best. The gun cracked and they were off and running. After the last curve the unthinkable happened. The United States was ahead by 10 meters with no real competition in sight. And then, with victory in their grasp, it happened. They dropped the baton. The thousands in the stands gasped in disbelief. The United States sleek, muscular, and fast as leopards, lost the race. Why? Someone *dropped the baton*.[59]

We need to be asking what God needs from us. What unique ministry could we have to our community and our world? What great dream has God planted within our hearts? And then we need to begin gathering our resources to do what God has called us to do in the knowledge that He will provide the means to accomplish what He has called us to do. What could possibly be more tragic than hearing God's call and not responding?

What is God calling us to be and to do as His people in this time and this place? We too often as Christians *drop the baton* in our service to the Lord. It is not a question of resources but a question of faith.

When Paul says, *"For everyone looks out for his own interests, not those of Jesus Christ"* (2:21), is he not saying that we have a tendency to look out for our own happiness and comfort rather than suffer pain and discomfort for the cause of Christ? It is too easy for us in our health and wealth society to put comfort first on our list of pursuits. Too often the idea of suffering for the cause of Christ becomes a choice if we have to, but not a daily choice when it is in conflict with our comfort and well-being.

---

[59] Dynamic Preaching, October 1999

The story of Job is an interesting example of a human perception of pain and suffering. When God called in his angels for a "business meeting," Satan crashed the party. Then he challenged God to put Job on trial (Job 1). So God met his challenge because He knew that Job was up to the test. The Scripture says,

> *The Lord said to Satan, 'Very well, then, he is in your hands; but you must spare his life.' So Satan went out from the presence of the Lord and afflicted Job with painful sores from the soles of his feet to the top of his head. Then Job took a piece of broken pottery and scraped himself with it as he sat among the ashes* (Job 2:6-8).

In the third chapter, Job proceeds to complain about his being born. And then it is as if he is saying, "Why am I being punished when I have not done anything wrong" (Job 7:20, 21)? And it is as if God is saying to him, "I am not punishing you, I am defending you." In other words, God is saying, "*Satan has challenged me in regards to your integrity!*" Job's problem here is a matter of perception. We would all probably feel like Job did at this point, because we often cannot see the purpose of pain and suffering other than it being a consequence of some sin we have committed or bad choice we have made.

God's sees the bigger picture. The Father had confidence in Job and was willing to allow him to suffer as an example of the endurance of the human spirit when motivated by a complete faith in the Creator. In chapters 38-41, God speaks, and as Job must be slinking into the ashes in shame, he understands that the great Creator is in charge and that his destiny is in good hands.

Job was learning that his suffering was *not about him*, but about future generations who would understand their suffering for the cause of Christ. Job was to be an example so that they might become emboldened to suffer for the FAITH. Job was to be an example of how God would be with them and empower them regardless of the suffering they might encounter.

We see Job reply and it finally dawns on him when he says,

> ... *I know that you can do all things; no plan of yours can be thwarted. You asked, 'Who is this that obscures my counsel without knowledge?' Surely I spoke of things I did not understand, things too wonderful for me to know. You said, 'Listen now, and I will speak; I will question you and you shall answer me.' My ears had heard of you but now my eyes have seen you. Therefore I despise myself and repent in dust and ashes* (Job 42:1-6).

So you see then that when TRUTH SEEKING trumps HAPPINESS SEEKING in the disciple's mindset, JOY is not only possible, it becomes a common emotion and spiritual condition in the believer's daily life.

The Church is an Organism

The apostle Paul declares that the church is an interdependent organism when he states,

> *The eye cannot say to the hand, 'I don't need you!' And the head cannot say to the feet, 'I don't need you!' On the contrary, those parts of the body that seem to be weaker are indispensable, and the parts that we think are less honorable we treat with*

special honor. And the parts that are unpresentable are treated with special modesty, while our presentable parts need no special treatment. But God has combined the members of the body and has given greater honor to the parts that lacked it, so that there should be no division in the body, but that its parts should have equal concern for each other. If one part suffers, every part suffers with it; if one part is honored, every part rejoices with it (1 Corinthians 12:21-26).

Paul is saying that no one who claims to be Christ's disciple should DROP THE BATON, but that we all should care for one another above concern for ourselves (2:3, 4). Dr. Paul Brand and Philip Yancey have written a wonderful book titled, *Fearfully and Wonderfully Made*. In their book, they make a comparison of the cellular organism of the body to the organism of the church.

Dr. Brand was a surgeon and cellular biologist, and he specialized in the field of pain and he worked in the leprosy hospital in Carville, Louisiana. Dr. Brand states,

> But the white cell contains granules of chemical explosives, and as soon as the bacteria are absorbed the granules detonate, destroying the invaders. In thirty seconds to a minute only the bloated white cell remains. Often its task is a kamikaze one, resulting in the white cell's own death.

He goes on to say,

> I sometimes think of the human body as a community, and then of its individual cells such as the white cell. The cell is the basic unit of an organism; it can live for itself, or it can help form and sustain the larger

organism. I recall the apostle Paul's use of an analogy in 1 Corinthians 12, where he compares the church of Christ to the human body.

Dr. Brand continues,

> That analogy conveys a more precise meaning to me because though a hand or foot or ear cannot have a life separate from the body, a cell does have that potential. It can be part of the body as a loyalist, or it can cling to its own life. Some cells do choose to live in the body, sharing its benefits while maintaining complete independence they become parasites or cancer cells.[60]

It is quite evident that the comparison is made between the cells in the physical body and the members in the church body. In other words, if a member decides to disengage in ministry, to not use his/her talents or gifts, the result is that the member allows himself/herself to be potentially a parasite, accepting the benefits of discipleship, but ultimately, slowly endangering the body of Christ and subjecting it to weakness and ineffectiveness. It is a case of having dropped the *baton*.

In this book by Brand and Yancey, a profound statement is made,

> The process of joining Christ's Body may at first seem like renunciation. I no longer have full independence. Ironically, however, renouncing my

---

[60] Paul Brand and Philip Yancey, *Fearfully and Wonderfully Made*, Zondervan Publishing House, 20

old value system in which I had to compete with other people on the basis of power, wealth, and talent and committing myself to Christ, the Head, abruptly frees me. My sense of competition fades. No longer do I have to bristle against life, seizing ways to prove myself. In my new identity my ideal has become to live my life in such a way that people around me recognize Jesus Christ and His love, not my own set of distinctive qualities. My worth and acceptance are enveloped in Him. I have found this process of renunciation and commitment to be healthy, relaxing and wholly good.[61]

It is only when we sacrifice self that we find the peace and joy God promises us.

Serving as Disciples of Christ

It was discovered that an anonymous man wrote a letter, back in the second century A.D., to a friend in which, he described these Christians, who were hated and harassed by their neighbors. He wrote,

> They marry and have children just like everyone else, but they do not kill unwanted babies. They offer a shared table but not a shared bed. They are passing their days on earth, but are citizens of heaven.

And listen to this next line: "They obey the appointed laws and *go beyond the laws in their own lives.*"

---

[61] Brand and Yancey, 48

Joyfully Serving as Christ's Disciple

"They love everyone," he continues,

> ... but are persecuted by all. They are put to death and gain life. They are poor and yet make many rich. They are dishonored and yet gain glory through dishonor. Their names are blackened and yet they are cleared. They are mocked and bless in return. They are treated outrageously and behave respectfully to others. When they do good they are punished as evildoers; when punished, they rejoice as if being given new life.[62]

There is a story told that reflects this same principle of servanthood. Brothers David and John Livingstone had very different goals for their lives. John dreamed of being rich and famous. From a young age, David dreamed of following Christ. Both boys achieved their goals.

John Livingstone became rich and famous. David Livingstone became a medical missionary to Africa. He was never rich, although he did become famous as one of the best-known missionaries of the 19th century.

In his later years, he was offered the chance to return to England as a hero and live out his last days in comfort. Here was his chance to bask in the admiration of the people! To reap the rewards from his many years of service! Instead, David chose to remain in Africa, where he lived in poverty. He died of a tropical disease. Both brothers lived out their dreams. And yet, on John Livingstone's tomb are engraved these words: "Here lies the brother of David Livingstone."[63]

Jesus said, *"...whoever wants to become great among you must be your servant, and whoever wants to be first must be*

---

[62] Dynamic Preaching, September 2001
[63] Michael P. Green, *Illustrated for Biblical Preaching*, Baker Book House, (1989) 131-132

your slave" (Matthew 20:26, 27). The saddest secret is that too many of us as Christians it seems have lost the desire to be humble and suffer for the cause of Christ.

In verse 20, Paul says of Timothy that he has no one like him who takes a "genuine interest" in the welfare of the Philippian church. Jackson says of this passage,

> The term 'care' (KJV) is of great interest. The verbal base is *merimnao*, which can mean to 'worry, be anxious,' or 'to take thought for, be concerned about.' In the New Testament, there is a *right* kind of anxiety and a *wrong* kind. For example, the 'cares' of this world can choke out the good seed from one's heart (Matthew 13:22), or the 'cares' of life can cause one to not be attentive to the return of Christ (Luke 21:34). Our 'cares' should be cast upon God (1 Peter 5:7). Christ cautions us not to 'take thought for' (i.e., worry about) the necessities of life, for God will see to our needs, even as He does His lower creatures (Matthew 6:25ff). In these passages 'care' (inordinate worry) is discouraged.
>
> On the other hand, Paul stresses that Christians need to have 'care' for one another, as members of the same body (1 Corinthians 12:25). In fact, 'anxiety' for all the churches was a daily pressing matter for the great apostle himself (2 Corinthians 11:28). It is thus a marvelous tribute to Timothy when Paul suggests that the young gentleman's 'care' for the Philippians is in a class of its own. Timothy was no hireling (cf. John 10:12, 13); he had a sterling concern for his brothers in the Lord.[64]

---

[64] Jackson, 93, 94

Overcoming our Environment

One of the biggest questions a disciple of Christ must ask himself is, do I give in to the pressures and stresses of my environment? We must demolish arguments and every pretension that sets itself up against the knowledge of God, and take captive every thought to make it obedient to Christ (2 Corinthians 10:5). Do we allow our environment to determine our joy or do we control our thoughts and keep them within the boundaries of hope in Jesus Christ?

Chuck Swindoll tells about a research psychologist at the National Institute of Mental Health who was concerned about the stresses of modern life. His name was John Calhoun. His theory was, "Overcrowded conditions take a terrible toll on humanity."

> Dr. Calhoun built a nine-foot square cage for his mice. He observed them closely as their population grew. He started with eight mice. The cage was designed to contain comfortably a population of 160. He allowed the mice to grow, however, to a population of 2200. They were not deprived of any of life's necessities except privacy; no time or space to be all alone. Food, water, and other resources were always clean and in abundance. A pleasant temperature was maintained. No disease was present. All mortality factors (except aging) were eliminated. The cage, except for its overcrowded condition, was ideal for the mice. The population reached its peak at 2200 after about two-and-a-half years. Since there was no way for the mice to physically escape from their closed environment, Dr. Calhoun was interested in how they would handle themselves. Interestingly, as the population reached its peak, the colony of mice

began to disintegrate. Strange stuff started happening. The males who had protected their territory withdrew from leadership. The females became aggressive and forced out the young . . . even their own offspring. The young grew to be only self-indulgent. They ate, drank, slept, groomed themselves, but showed no normal aggression and, most noteworthy, failed to reproduce. After five years, every mouse had died. This occurred despite the fact that right up to the end there was plenty of food, water, and absence of disease.[65]

This is a parable of modern life. For many people, a simple task like getting to work is extremely draining. There are too many cars on the highway. Commuting time is getting longer. Driving a car, sitting in front of a computer screen, working all day long with clients, and other stressful pursuits can only drain us of our JOY. But if we allow the stresses of life to control us, we will miss out on the blessings that Christ has in store for us. As His disciples, we can do all things through Christ, even overcome our environment (4:13).

---

[65] Dynamic Preaching, January 2003

Questions for Review

1. How would you define a disciple of Christ?
2. How would you define the concept The Church is an Organism?
3. How does Christ define a servant in Matthew 20?
4. How should we overcome our environment?
5. What did Dr. Brand say about the human cell?
6. How did Brand compare the human cell to a member of the church body?
7. What was wrong with Job's perspective on his pain and suffering?
8. Why did God feel the need to respond to Satan's challenge of Job?

Lesson Eight
(Chapter 3:1-11)

Joyfully Knowing Christ Personally

Finally, my brothers, rejoice in the Lord! It is not trouble for me to write the same things to you again, and it is a safeguard for you.

Watch out for those dogs, those men who do evil, those mutilators of the flesh. For it is we who are the circumcision, we who worship by the Spirit of God, who glory in Christ Jesus, and who put no confidence in the flesh though I myself have reason for such confidence.

If anyone else thinks he has reasons to put confidence in the flesh, I have more: circumcised on the eighth day of the people of Israel, of the tribe of Benjamin, a Hebrew of Hebrews; in regard to the law, a Pharisee; as for zeal, persecuting the church; as for legalistic righteousness, faultless.

But whatever was to my profit I now consider loss for the sake of Christ. What is more, I consider everything a loss compared to the surpassing greatness of knowing Christ Jesus my Lord, for whose sake I have lost all things. I consider them rubbish, that I may gain Christ and be found in him, not having a righteousness of my own that comes from the law, but that which is through faith in Christ the righteousness that comes from God and is by faith. I

> want to know Christ and the power of his resurrection and the fellowship of sharing in his sufferings, becoming like him in his death, and so, somehow, to attain to the resurrection from the dead.

A fable cites the case of the unfortunate frog caught in a deep rut on a country road. His frog friends tried to rescue him but finally gave up in despair. However, the next day the frog was out of the rut and hopping about. Said a friendly frog, "I thought you were stuck in that rut and couldn't get out." To which he received the reply, "That's right. I couldn't. But a truck came along and I had to." (Author unknown)

It's amazing what we can do when we have to. Motivation is the key. Life has many ruts and all of us some time or another find ourselves stuck, but with proper motivation, we can find a way out. Of course it takes motivation to know Christ personally; it doesn't just happen automatically or by osmosis.

Jackson explains,

> The apostle had been willing to suffer the loss of all things for the following reasons. First, he says, it was that he might 'know him [Christ], and the power of his resurrection.' The term 'know' suggests the idea of obtaining more personal knowledge of the Lord by *experience*. It underscores the influence of the one 'known' upon him who comes to 'know.' The reference to the 'power of his resurrection' is an affirmation of the significance of that historical event in the life of this apostle. The fact of the resurrection had been the propelling force behind Paul's

conversion; that event also was an abiding influence in the apostle's ongoing life.[66]

It is interesting that there are two primary Greek words that are translated *know* in the New Testament. They are *ginosko* and *oida*. The Greek word *ginosko* is used in 3:10 and is translated "know." W. E. Vine states,

> The differences between *ginosko* and *oida* demand consideration: *ginosko*, frequently suggests inception or progress in knowledge, while *oida* suggests fullness of knowledge. In the New Testament *ginosko* frequently indicates a relation between the person knowing and the object known; in this respect, what is known is of value or importance to the one who knows, and hence the establishment of the relationship. The Greek word *oida* signifies primarily, to have seen or perceived; hence, to know, to have knowledge of; in the case of human knowledge, to know from observation.[67]

This same word, *ginosko*, is used in Matthew 1:25, indicating an "intimate knowledge" of a person. In this case, Joseph did not "know" (have sexual relations with) Mary until Jesus was born. This same root Greek word, *ginosko*, is found in Matthew 7:23. In other words, Jesus is saying that no matter what we do in the name of Christ, if we don't "know" him intimately, we will be considered as "evildoers!"

---

[66] Jackson, 118
[67] Vine's, 638

One commentator explains it this way in reference to Matthew 7:23;

> It should be observed that Jesus defines 'doing the will of God' (7:21) in terms of one's relationship to himself ('I never knew you'; 7:23). Jesus is thus ascribing to himself a decisive role in determining one's eternal welfare. As the proclaimer and doer of the perfect will of God, Jesus exemplifies both the demand and promise of God's covenant with his people.[68]

It would seem then that "knowing" Christ intimately is more important than having knowledge of him, even more than doing good works in His name. It is true then that without a personal relationship with Him, we are without hope. That is why Paul wanted to KNOW Jesus personally, and the power of His resurrection. It is a personal relationship that transcends simple knowledge about Him. It is intimately learning more of Jesus' example and power in the life of a disciple.

Evaluating our Past

In this text, Paul evaluates or assesses his life. Socrates said, "The unexamined life is not worth living." Many people today are slaves of "things" and as a result do not experience real Christian joy. Paul is saying, "Have no confidence in works of righteousness." In contrast he is saying that true Christians are described as those who: 1) worship God in

---

[68] Larry Chouinard, *The College Press NIV Commentary on Matthew*, College Press Publishing Company, 145

spirit and truth, 2) boast in Jesus Christ, and 3) and have no confidence in the flesh.

Paul had everything going for him in his relation to the Law and the nation of Israel. But knowing Christ was more valuable. To have an intimate relationship with Jesus Christ was more valuable. Someone said, "We give up what we can't KEEP for what we can't LOSE!" Paul contrasted what he used to be with what he presently was (1 Timothy 1:12-17).

Paul did not look back to gloat on his accomplishments, or to compare himself with others (2 Corinthians 10:12). He only looked ahead. Jesus said to *"keep your hand on the plow and don't look back"* (Luke 9:62). He was pressing on, letting God work in and through him. Someone said, "Direction determines destination." It is not enough to run hard and win the race, because we must obey the rules. We must make a conscious decision to run the race. We are not in competition with others in this race. Paul did not worry about finishing FIRST, SECOND or THIRD in the race. He simply said, "DON'T LOOK BACK!" We just need to finish the race (2 Timothy 4:6-8). When we finish the race faithful to Christ it won't matter when we come in, for there is no competition with anybody else in this race (Galatians 6:4).

The Fellowship of Suffering

Philip Yancey, the well-respected author of the book *Where is God When It Hurts*, has spent time he says with many servants who have experienced the fellowship of suffering.

> People like Dr. Paul Brand, who worked for twenty years among the poorest of the poor, leprosy patients in rural India; or health workers who left high paying jobs to serve with Mendenhall Ministries in a

backwater town of Mississippi; or relief workers in Somalia, Sudan, Ethiopia, Bangladesh, or other such repositories of world-class human suffering; or the Ph.D.'s scattered through jungles of South America translating the Bible into obscure languages.

Yancey says he was prepared to honor and admire these servants, to hold them up as inspiring examples. He was not, however, prepared to envy them. But as he now reflects on the two groups side by side,

> ... stars and servants, the servants clearly emerge as the favored ones the graced ones. They work for low pay, long hours, and no applause, 'wasting' their talents and skills among the poor and uneducated. But somehow in the process of losing their lives they have found them. They received the 'peace that is not of this world.'

Yancey goes on to say that when he thinks of the great churches he has visited,

> What comes to mind is not an image of a cathedral in Europe. These are mere museums now. Instead, he thinks ...of an inner-city church in Newark with crumbling plaster and a leaky roof, of a mission church in Santiago, Chile, made of concrete block and corrugated iron. In these places, set amidst human misery, he says he has seen Christian love abound.[69]

We may or may not agree with Yancey's doctrinal stance on any one subject, but it is apparent in this world that there

---

[69] Philip Yancey, *Where is God When it Hurts*, 51

are some who experience the fellowship of suffering with others who suffer, and their joy is genuine and powerful. I wonder if this is what Paul is saying when he says that he gave up all he had attained and counted it as rubbish to simply know Christ and somehow experience the fellowship of sharing in his sufferings.

Barclay states,

> It means to know the *fellowship of his sufferings.* Again and again, Paul returns to the thought that, when Christians have to suffer, they are in some strange way sharing the very suffering of Christ and are even filling up that suffering. It means to be so united with Christ that day by day we come more to share in his death, so that finally we share the way he walked; we share the cross he bore; we share the death he died; and finally we share the life he lives for evermore.

He continues,

> To know Christ is not to be skilled in any theoretical or theological knowledge; it is to know him with such intimacy that in the end we are as united with him as we are with those whom we love on earth, and that, just as we share their experiences, so we also share his.[70]

Malone concurs when he says,

> It is knowing *him*–not just facts about him–that changed Paul's life. Nikita Khrushchev [premier of Communist Russia] as a boy won prizes repeatedly from a parish priest because of his remarkable ability to

---

[70] Barclay, 76

quote the gospels. Anyone familiar with his life and his leadership in the Soviet system knows that Khrushchev did not in reality accept the very words which he could quote so amazingly. It is one thing to know facts and another thing altogether to know Christ.[71]

Our Purpose

Douglas Parsons writes about the story of Carl A. Boyle, titled *More Than One Cup.*

> Carl A. Boyle, a sales representative, was driving home when he saw a group of young children selling Kool-Aid on a corner in a neighborhood. They had posted the typical handscrawled sign over their stand: 'Kool-Aid, 10 cents.' Carl was intrigued. He pulled over to the curb. A young man approached and asked if he would like strawberry or grape Kool-Aid. Carl placed his order and handed the boy a quarter. After much deliberation, the children determined he had some change coming and rifled through the cigar box until they finally came up with the correct amount. The boy returned with the change, as they stood by the side of the car. He asked if Carl was finished drinking. 'Just about,' said Carl. 'Why?' 'That's the only cup we have,' answered the boy, 'and we need it to stay in business.'

Parsons goes on to say,

> It's difficult to operate a Kool-Aid business if you only have one cup. We sometimes make that mistake in the church. Evangelism is more than an occasional

---

[71] Malone, 83

gospel meeting or canvassing door-to-door or passing out tracts. By limiting our vision of the evangelistic thrust of the church to two or three cups, we deprive ourselves of one of the most rewarding opportunities Christ Jesus offers us.

Matthew writes that Jesus *'saw the crowds and had compassion for them, because they were harassed and helpless, like sheep without a shepherd'* (Matthew 9:36). Can you think of a better description of the mass of people today harassed like sheep without a shepherd? There are families that are disintegrating, young minds being destroyed by drugs, old folks feeling forgotten. The need is overwhelming.

Our goal as a church is not to enhance institutional pride. Our motive is not a more impressive bottom line. Our aim is not to be the biggest and the best. Our purpose is to be the body of Christ in this place.

Jesus had compassion on the crowds. Harassed and helpless they were like sheep without a shepherd. And there were so many of them. Just like today. The harvest is plentiful; but the laborers are few. Where are the laborers? Where are those who care enough to become involved in the lives of others? Where are those who are willing to take their time to show love to young people and old folks, to the substance abuser and the victims of broken families, to the down-and-out as well as the up-and-in? It's going to take a lot of cups. Jesus Christ is still asking, 'Where are the laborers?' Can He count on you?

It is evident that Jesus, continually in his ministry, was willing to fellowship with the suffering of others. His example in this aspect of ministry defines then our purpose in ministry. It is true that our prime goal is to spread the gospel, but our purpose is also to seek fellowship with the suffering of others that we might lead them to Christ Jesus. Paul became all things to others that he might save some (1 Corinthians 9:19-23).

It would seem then that this is what Paul had in mind when he said that he wanted to *know* Jesus and *share* in the fellowship of his sufferings. In fact, we should expect as His disciples who desire to live a godly life, we will share in His sufferings.

Frame of Mind

In their book, *Happiness is a Choice*, Drs. Frank Minirth and Paul Meier, establish the fact that our mindset determines our happiness. Their thesis is that depression too often is a choice and since it is a mental choice, we can choose not to get depressed. I believe that JOY is a choice if we are willing to trust God and suffer with our Lord Jesus Christ.

In his book, *Living Life on Purpose*, Greg Anderson shares the story of one man's journey.

> His wife had left him and he was in deep depression. He had lost faith in himself, in other people, and in God he could find no joy in living.
>
> One rainy morning this man went to a small neighborhood restaurant for breakfast. Although several people were at the diner, no one was speaking to anyone else. Our miserable friend hunched over the counter, lost in thought as he stirred his coffee.
>
> In one of the small booths along the window was a young mother with a little girl. They had just been

served their food when the little girl broke the sad silence by almost shouting, 'Momma, why don't we say our prayers here?'

The waitress who had just served their breakfast turned around and said, 'Sure, honey, we pray here. Will you say the pray for us?' And the little girl turned and looked at the rest of the people in the restaurant and said, 'Bow your heads.'

Surprisingly, one by one, the heads went down. The little girl then bowed her head, folded her hands, and said, 'God is great, God is good, and we thank Him for our food. Amen.'

That prayer changed the entire atmosphere. People began to talk with one another. The waitress said, 'We should do that every morning.' Anderson recalls, that his friend said, 'All of a sudden, I started to thank God for all that I did have and stop focusing on all that I didn't have. I started to choose happiness.'

This is why Paul could rejoice in the Lord, because he knew that such JOY was a frame of mind and that suffering with Christ was not so much a duty, but a privilege and that the rewards out-weighed the pain and afflictions. I wish all Christians who claim to be true disciples, would embrace this vital element (frame of mind) for securing not only joy but the assurance of eternity. The apostle John tells us that, *"I write these things to you who believe in the name of the Son of God so that you may know that you have eternal life"* (1 John 5:13).

Questions for Review

1. How did Paul know Jesus intimately?
2. How can we know Jesus intimately?
3. What are the values and the dangers of evaluating the past?
4. What does the concept of Fellowship of Suffering mean?
5. What is the difference between the two Greek words *ginosko and oida*?
6. What was the main point in the story by Douglas Parsons?
7. What is the meaning of the phrase, "We give up what we can't keep for what we can't lose?"
8. What does Socrates mean when he said, "The unexamined life is not worth living?"

Lesson Nine
(Chapter 3:12-16)

Joyfully Pressing Toward the Goal

Not that I have already obtained all this, or have already been made perfect, but I press on to take hold of that for which Christ Jesus took hold of me. Brothers, I do not consider myself yet to have taken hold of it. But one thing I do: Forgetting what is behind and straining toward what is ahead, I press on toward the goal to win the prize for which God has called me heavenward in Christ Jesus.

All of us who are mature should take such a view of things. And if on some point you think differently, that too God will make clear to you. Only let us live up to what we have already attained.

Albert Einstein once wrote,

I was once asked if I could ask God one question, 'What would it be?' I answered that I would ask how the universe began, because once I knew that, the rest was simple mathematics. But now, on second thought, I would not ask God *how* the universe began. Rather, I would want to know *why* he started the universe. For once I knew that, then, I would know the purpose of my own life.

In reference to the *goal* Paul is talking about in this segment of Philippians, one commentator states,

> This is a race in which all finishers are winners. Yet this does not diminish the effort of the runner, for the course (like a marathon) is such that even to finish is an achievement. The Greek term translated 'goal' (*skopos*, literally 'goal marker') is found only here in the New Testament. The prize is not defined, but would include all that is involved in complete fellowship with God beyond the restrictions encountered in this life.[72]

What is our goal in our Christian walk? Is it to simply attend worship services two or three times a week? It is so easy to delude ourselves that by coming to worship once or twice a week, we have fulfilled our commitment to Christ. Worship is where we prepare ourselves for service outside the church building.

> In 2001, Allison Levine led the first all-woman team to climb Mt. Everest. Allison is a particularly inspiring leader, because for much of her life she was unable to take on any physical challenges. Born with a heart defect, Allison never played sports or rough-housed like other kids her age. Any exertion could cause her heart to jump out of its regular rhythm. At the age of 30, Allison underwent surgery to repair her heart defect. Afterwards, she became a dedicated athlete.

---

[72] Anthony L. Ash, *The College Press NIV Commentary, Philippians, Colossians, Philemon,* College Press, 103

Allison agreed to lead the Mt. Everest expedition with one stipulation: that the climb would be a fund-raising effort to raise money for good causes, like cancer research and for building girls' schools in Nepal. She didn't want to climb Everest for her own or the team's glory; she wanted the team to give back something to those less fortunate. As Allison Levine said, 'What's the point of taking such risks if nothing changes on the earth below?'[73]

Paul's thinking was of such a nature that he saw everything in a spiritual perspective. In other words, the prize was the goal because the prize is of such a nature that nothing on this earth can compare. It is so hard for us as human beings to make such a comparison. We often look at our world and see that there is a gradual process of depravity, but yet we, in general, enjoy this life too much to change our goals from the satisfaction of the flesh to embracing the prize of heaven. We too often are not willing to pay the price of suffering and endurance for the sake of gaining such a prize.

Lot's Story

I am reminded of the story of Lot and his family in the book of Genesis. It is recorded that,

> *Abram said to Lot, 'Let's not have any quarreling between you and me, or between your herdsmen and mine, for we are brothers. Is not the whole land before you? Let's part company. If you go to the left,*

---

[73] Diane Hales, *The Climb of Her Dreams*, Lifetime, December 2003/January 2004, 79-81

I'll go to the right; if you go to the right, I'll go to the left.'

Lot looked up and saw that the whole plain of the Jordan was well watered, like the garden of the Lord, like the land of Egypt, toward Zoar, (This was before the Lord destroyed Sodom and Gomorrah). So Lot chose for himself the whole plain of the Jordan and set out toward the east. The two men parted company: Abram lived in the land of Canaan, while Lot lived among the cities of the plain and pitched his tents near Sodom. Now the men of Sodom were wicked and were sinning greatly against the Lord (Genesis 13:8-13).

What was Lot thinking? Did he not know that the city of Sodom was full of wickedness and sinfulness? Did he not know that his decision put his family in danger? Did he not know that he could have lost his soul? I know that the apostle Peter said of Lot,

... Lot, a righteous man, who was distressed by the filthy lives of lawless men (for that righteous man, living among them day after day, was tormented in his righteous soul by the lawless deeds he saw and heard)... (2 Peter 2:7-8).

Again, why did Lot make the decision to move there when he must have known that it would put him and his family in spiritual and moral danger? Is it not a classic example of choosing HAPPINESS SEEKING over TRUTH SEEKING?

When we look at the example of Lot it is easy to criticize him for his wanting to enjoy the pleasures and benefits of a beautiful and financially prosperous land. But do we not make such decisions every day? Our tendency is to seek out opportunities to live better and more comfortable even if we know it might be at the cost of our family's spiritual needs and the potential of their being unfaithful to the Lord Jesus Christ. What is the goal of our lives?

The Good, the Bad, and the Phony

The apostle Paul is telling us that he had given up all that was to his profit and considered it loss (garbage) for the sake of Christ (3:7). It reminds me again of the time Jesus was preaching about the need for disciples to eat His flesh and drink His blood (John 6:60-71). The sermon on the bread of life produced decisive effects. It converted popular enthusiasm for Jesus into disgust. It separated true from false disciples, and like a winnowing breeze, it blew the chaff away, leaving a residue of wheat behind. John records, *"From this time many of his disciples turned back and no longer followed him. 'You do not want to leave too, do you?' Jesus asked the Twelve"* (John 6:67).

Yet, however greatly tempted to forsake their Master, the Twelve did abide faithfully by His side. They did come safely through the spiritual storm. Why did Jesus make such a statement? Surely He knew that these words would be interpreted as revolting and that it was not a good political move. The Twelve were probably wondering why He would say such things. It is very much like when Jesus spoke in parables, and His disciples thought it was not wise if He were going to win a following (Matthew 13). It seems as though Jesus was seeking to separate the disciples who followed Him for the physical food He had provided, from those disciples who sought truth over happiness.

Yet, the secret to the steadfastness of the Twelve

(actually the Eleven since Judas was without sincere motives) would be the anchors that provided them the strength to ride out the storm. Their supreme desire was to know *"the words of eternal life;"* actually to gain possession of life (John 6:63), or might I say to choose *truth above happiness.* Their concern was not about the meat that perishes, but about the higher heavenly food of the soul. They became disciples not to better their worldly circumstances, but to obtain eternity, and the benefits of such, which the world could neither give them nor take from them.

In Judas' case, a little religion will carry a man through many trials, but there is usually a crisis or two coming which nothing but sincerity can stand. When he had to make a decision on the basis of pleasure and happiness, he caved in to the joys of this life. He had a religion, but not a relationship with Jesus Christ.

Peter obviously had already considered his options. *"To whom shall we go?"* asked Peter. Was heathenism a viable alternative with its immorality and cruelty? Was Judaism the answer with its hypocrisy, superficiality and legalism? Was worldliness the key with its hopelessness and indifference? What about John the Baptist? If he were alive, wouldn't he simply again point them to Jesus?

They had been with Jesus long enough. They had seen His miracles, experienced His marvelous wisdom, and received His wonderful grace and mercy. They had witnessed His rejection of falsehood, pride, vanity and tyranny. They had experienced a blessed fellowship and ministry with Him. All this had begotten a confidence too strong to be shaken by a single address containing some statements hard to understand.

They had all the facts they needed to put His truth and power above their comfort, wealth, status and welfare. What would you and I have done in such a circumstance, and we were called upon to declare our allegiance to Jesus? Would we have gone with the crowd or stayed with the Twelve? My guess is that if we had lived a life of putting *happiness above truth*, we would have gone with the crowd.

The Law of Obedience

Paul is not saying that he needs someone to help him feel better about himself when he talks about all he has given up. He is trying to tell us that it is his life's goal to be obedient to the higher discipline of his Master. Then Paul could enjoy the peace and contentment of knowing he was committed to the Master.

In Jack London's classic story, *White Fang*, the point London makes is that this dog is half dog half wolf. After living in the wild, he is domesticated and learns to live among people. White Fang was very fond of chickens. On one occasion he raided a chicken roost and killed fifty hens. His master, Weeden Scott, scolded him and then took him into the chicken yard.

There he placed White Fang right in the middle of the chickens. This was a supreme test. When White Fang saw his favorite food walking around right in front of him he obeyed his natural impulse and lunged for a chicken. He was immediately checked by his master's voice. They stayed in the chicken yard for quite a while, and every time White Fang made a move toward a chicken, his master's voice would stop him. In this way he learned what his master wanted; he had learned to ignore the chickens.

Weeden Scott's father argued that you "couldn't cure a chicken killer," but Weeden challenged him and they agreed to lock White Fang in with the chickens all afternoon. Listen as Jack London describes the scene:

Locked in the yard and there deserted by the master, White Fang lay down and went to sleep. Once he got up and walked over to the trough for a drink of water. The chickens he calmly ignored. So far as he was concerned they did not exist. At four o'clock he executed a running jump, gained the roof of the chicken house, and leaped to the ground outside, whence he sauntered gravely to the house.

Then Jack London adds these words: "He had learned the Law." What law was that? It is the law of obedience. White Fang moved from following the dictates of his own natural cravings to being obedient to the higher discipline of his master. He learned to elevate truth over happiness. He learned to respect, and honor the master's law. He then could enjoy the peace and contentment of obedience to the law. Why is it that humans have such a hard time learning this basic truth. Maybe it is because humans have a hard time accepting their Master. Too often we as humans want to be our own master.

Again Jackson comments: "Paul states that he is 'stretching forward' toward the goal. His aim is to obtain 'the prize' of the high calling in Christ Jesus. The source of the calling is God. It is humble in attitude. It's medium is through the gospel. Its design is holiness. Its direction is upward. Its sphere is Christ, and its hope is one with a focus upon heaven."[74]

The Peril of the Temporal Life

Paul is committed to the truth that this world is passing and all that is in it. That this world is temporal and all the

---

[74] Jackson, 124

pursuits of the human race, unless dictated by an obedience to Jesus Christ, are futile.

Rick Marschall is the author of more than 60 books and hundreds of magazine articles in many fields, from pop culture to history and criticism. He writes in his blog (mondayministry.com) of a writer by the name Whittaker Chambers. Chambers lived a life of profound impact, Marschall says, of brilliant achievements politically as he affected American life through his writings. From Chambers' book, *Witness* (1952), he quotes Chambers saying,

> Human societies, like human beings, live by faith and die when faith dies. The communist vision is the vision of man without God. A man is not primarily a witness against something. That is only incidental to the fact that he is witness for something. I know that I am leaving the winning side [Communism] for the losing side [freedom], but it is better to die on the losing side than to live under Communism.

He goes on to say,

> The rub is that the pursuit of happiness, as an end in itself, tends automatically, and widely, to be replaced by the pursuit of pleasure with a consequent general softening of the fibers of will, intelligence, spirit. When you understand what you see, you will no longer be children. You will know that life is pain, that each of us hangs always upon the cross of himself. And when you know that this is true of every man, woman and child on earth, you will be wiser. I see in Communism the focus of the concentrated evil of our time.

I quote from Marschall's account and his quote from the book, *Witness*, because of the tremendous impact that Whittaker Chambers had on many people and this nation in the 1940's and 50's. I am impressed with Whittaker's journey from a hard core Communist to a believer in the reality of God and the freedom such faith brings. His conclusions in his writings on the world and life in general, are impressive and they substantiate the fact that the goal of *happiness seeking* in this life is an illusion. Only in the pursuit of TRUTH, even though painful and uncomfortable at times, is the life of faith, purpose and hope to be found, and only in Christ Jesus.

Life without Bitterness

It is amazing to see the apostle Paul face persecution and then, as he writes this letter to the Philippian church, that only joy fills his heart, only persistence and faith control his words, only an undying faith in his Master motivates him.

Dr. Thomas Lambit, a medical missionary in Africa, was fascinated when he first saw African citizens crossing through turbulent rivers to get to their destination. There were very few bridges over these rivers, yet local citizens had no problem walking through the rushing water and over slippery rocks. You see, they had worked out a fool-proof way to remain sure-footed in a slippery situation: each citizen, before crossing the river, would pick up the largest, heaviest stone he could carry. This stone would weigh a person down enough that it would keep his feet firmly planted. He could stand securely because of his extra burden.[75]

Someone said in reference to trials and burdens, "Don't

---

[75] Ruth Peters, *Illustrations of Bible Truths*, compiled by Peters and published by AMG Publishers, 252

wish it were easier, wish you were better." It is a cliché, but nevertheless it is true. Hardship serves either to make us bitter or to make us better. The choice is ours. But we need to know this: There is no future in bitterness. Bitterness never motivated anyone to a higher plane of life. We can move to a higher plane of life, but first of all, we are going to have to face some challenges, hardships, and adversity. What's true in physical accomplishments is also true in the spiritual life: no pain, no gain. We admire overcomers. Hardships are necessary for emotional and spiritual maturity. Hardships remind us of our need for God.

The Hebrew writer said of hardships and discipline:

Endure hardship as discipline; God is treating you as sons. For what son is not disciplined by his father? If you are not disciplined (and everyone undergoes discipline), then you are illegitimate children and not true sons. Moreover, we have all had human fathers who disciplined us and we respected them for it. How much should we submit to the Father of our spirits and live! Our fathers disciplined us for a little while as they thought best; but God disciplines us for our good, that we may share in his holiness. No discipline seems pleasant at the time, but painful. Later on, however, it produces a harvest of righteousness and peace for those who have been trained by it (Hebrews 12:7-11).

There are many people today who look into the future and the future looks bleak and unpromising. Let's be candid about it. Life can have heartaches and many dark and terrifying moments. If you have ever lost someone you loved, if you have ever sat in a doctor's office and heard him pronounce a death sentence, if you have ever asked questions like, how can I ever pay my health insurance premiums with no job? What will the children do with no father? Am I destined to live my life with no hope of bettering my situation? These questions can be debilitating.

Isn't it interesting that Paul does not dwell on such questions of living in this world. He is totally consumed with the life to come. Malone states,

> As Paul saw it, the Christian is the athlete of Christ. At the outset of verse 13 Paul reiterates what he has just said (v. 12):
>
> *I count not myself yet to have laid hold. No perfectionism at this point for Paul. There must be no lagging in the race-running. '...But one thing I do, forgetting the things that are behind...'*
>
> This latter expression ('the things that are behind') looks back to the things mentioned in verses 5 and 6. Those religious attainments which, at one time, would have been grounds for glorying are now forgotten. Not that all memory of them has been totally eradicated (Paul has just mentioned them!), but in terms of his case before God, all of that is forgotten. No backward glances for Paul. Like the good runner, Paul with a single-minded, undiverted focus looks only ahead.[76]

Thus we see the reason Paul can JOYFULLY press on towards the goal of death, knowing that he is in good hands with his Lord. There is nothing else in this world that can

---

[76] Malone, 90

give man such confidence. The Bible tells us that, *"The fool says in his heart, there is no God"* (Psalms 14:1). Some may believe that there is no life after death. Who has the authority or the experience to consciously confirm the truth of that belief system? Paul says, I don't have to gamble with such a belief, *"I know whom I have believed, and am convinced that he is able to guard what I have entrusted to him for that day"* (2 Timothy 1:12).

Questions for Review

1. What is the prize that Paul is seeking?
2. When Whittaker Chambers said he left the winning side for the losing side, what did he mean?
3. How would you describe Lot's condition in your own words?
4. Why do you think Jesus said some things hard to understand?
5. What does the Law of Obedience mean?
6. Why is the goal of dying positive?
7. What do you suppose would have happened if Abram had chosen the well-watered plain of Jordan and Lot chose the land of Canaan?
8. What is the peril of the temporal life?

Lesson Ten
(Chapter 3:17-21)

Joyfully Transforming into Christ

Join with others in following my example, brothers, and take note of those who live according to the pattern we gave you. For, as I have often told you before and now say again even with tears, many live as enemies of the cross of Christ. Their destiny is destruction, their god is their stomach, and their glory is in their shame. Their mind is on earthly things. But our citizenship is in heaven. And we eagerly await a Savior from there, the Lord Jesus Christ, who, by the power that enables him to bring everything under his control, will transform our bodies so that they will be like his glorious body.

Christian philosopher C. S. Lewis once wrote,

The real test of being in the presence of God is that you either forget about yourself altogether or see yourself as a small dirty object. In God you come up against something which is in every respect immeasurably superior to yourself. Unless you know God as that and, therefore, know yourself as nothing by comparison you do not know God at all.

Jesus came to bring the NEW, not patch up the OLD (Luke 5:35-39). He is a *transformer* not a *reformer*. In these days of sanforized fabrics, and glass and plastic bottles, the illustration about cloth and wineskins may confuse some. The Jews of Jesus' day did not have pre-shrunk cloth for their clothing, and they frequently kept their liquids in animal skins. If a woman sewed a patch on a garment that had already been washed, the next time it was washed the patch would shrink and ruin both the patch and the garment. If new wine was poured into dry, brittle skins, the pressure on the gases from fermentation would break the skin and the wine would be lost.

With these illustrations, Christ taught how to relate to the old and to the new. Everything about Christ is new and everything that God wants us in Christ to be is new. The apostle Paul said, *"Therefore, if anyone is in Christ, he is a **new creation**; the old has gone, the new has come"* (2 Corinthians 5:17)!

Many Christians reject all things new. As a result, they lack the JOY and the POWER God has for them. Other Christians accept everything new and in the process, they destroy the old that must be preserved.

The Pharisees resisted change. The Lord was a threat to them because He released a new life in those who trusted Him. In their zeal to be *conservative* the Pharisees became *preservative* and fought the very things that were good for them. They had so embalmed their traditions that the people could not find the living Word. Jesus did not come to reform them or mankind in general. He came to transform them to a new life.

He transformed the old so that it is fulfilled in the new. If I have an acorn, I can destroy it either by a hammer or by planting it. In one instance it is ended totally, in the other it dies to produce an oak tree. In other words, the acorn is destroyed in fulfilling its purpose. Just as the old Law of Moses was fulfilled, died, and in the process allowed the new to spring up; we need to let old traditions of man to die, if they are no longer effective, and allow new, effective methods to spring up.

There is something about us that resists change, "we've always done it that way," is the theme song of many Christians. Instead of our churches ministering as TRANSFORMING fellowships, they muddle along monitoring CONFORMITY. Is this what Christ would want?

Paul also contends that we should not be *conformed* to this life, but be *transformed* by the renewing of the mind (Romans 12:2). This process requires the willingness of the mind to change and accept the truth of becoming more and more like Christ. Only such a transformation will provide us the power to experience the joy of this life, and the joy of changing our bodies to be like His glorious body in the life to come. Paul reminds us of the fact that we are not citizens of this world, but even now we are citizens of heaven.

Malone says,

> In contrast to the enemies of the cross, the Philippians are the privileged citizens of Christ's heavenly kingdom. Moffatt translates superbly: 'We are a colony of heaven.' Philippi, being a Roman colony (Acts 16:11, 12), was a little bit of Rome 'A Rome away from Rome.' Roman citizenship always appreciated was highly prized in the Roman colony. It is as if Paul is saying, 'I know you treasure your Roman citizenship, but ours is an incomparably greater citizenship calling us to lofty privileges and awesome responsibility.'[77]

---

[77] Malone, 96, 97

Our Bodies will Change

Paul is telling us that the enemies of Christ will be judged and that, *"Their destiny is destruction, their god is their stomach, and their glory is in their shame..."* (vs. 19) Jackson reminds us,

> In contrast, Paul reminds his faithful brethren: 'Our citizenship is in heaven.' Paul is contrasting the attitude of the spiritual with those who are constantly thinking on earthly things. The reason the true Christian rivets his thoughts on heaven is because from that holy sphere we are expecting, waiting for a Savior, Jesus Christ. When Christ comes, He will 'fashion anew' the body of our humiliation. The hope for the body is that it may be 'conformed' to the body of Christ's glory (i.e., the body of His glorified state). Christ was glorified following His resurrection, and so we shall be as well.[78]

When William Montague Dyke was ten years old, he was blinded in an accident.

> Despite his disability, William graduated from a university in England with high honors. While he was in school, he fell in love with the daughter of a high-ranking British naval officer, and they became engaged.

> Not long before the wedding, William had eye surgery in the hope that the operation would restore his sight. If it failed, he would remain blind for the

---

[78] Jackson, 128

rest of his life. William insisted on keeping the bandages on his face until his wedding day. If the surgery was successful, he wanted the first person he saw to be his new bride.

The wedding day arrived. The many guests including royalty, cabinet members, and distinguished men and women of society assembled together to witness the exchange of vows. William's father, Sir William Hart Dyke, and the doctor who performed the surgery stood next to the groom, whose eyes were still covered with bandages. The organ trumpeted the wedding march, and the bride slowly walked down the aisle to the front of the church. As soon as she arrived at the altar, the surgeon took a pair of scissors out of his pocket and cut the bandages from William's eyes. Tension filled the room. The congregation of witnesses held their breath as they waited to find out if William could see the woman standing before him. As he stood face-to-face with his bride-to-be, William's words echoed throughout the cathedral, 'You are more beautiful than I ever imagined!'

Author Kent Crocket, who tells this story in his book, *Making Today Count for Eternity*, writes:

One day the bandages that cover our eyes will be removed. When we stand face-to-face with Jesus Christ and see His face for the very first time, His glory will be far more splendid than anything we have ever imagined in this life.[79]

---

[79] Frank Lyman, edited this article, entitled *General Hospital*, commenting on John 9:1-25

We cannot possibly understand what Jesus' glorious body looks like. We can imagine though that it is beautiful and eternal. Paul describes our resurrection transformation this way;

> *So it will be with the resurrection of the dead. The body that is sown is perishable, it is raised imperishable; it is sown in dishonor, it is raised in glory; it is sown in weakness, it is raised in power; it is sown a natural body, it is raised a spiritual body. The spiritual did not come first, but the natural, and after that the spiritual. The first man was of the dust of the earth, the second man from heaven. As was the earthly man, so are those who are of the earth; and as is the man from heaven, so also are those who are of heaven. And just as we have borne the likeness of the earthly man, so shall we bear the likeness of the man from heaven* (1 Corinthians 15:42-44; 46-49).

Barclay describes it this way;

> Paul finishes with the Christian hope. Christians await the coming of Christ, at which everything will be changed. Here, the Authorized Version [KJV] is dangerously misleading. In verse 21, it speaks about our *vile body*. In modern speech, that would mean that the body is an utterly evil and horrible thing; but *vile* in sixteenth-century English still retained the meaning of its derivation from the Latin word *vilis*, which in fact means nothing worse than *cheap, valueless*. As we are now, our bodies are subject to change and decay, illness and death, the bodies of a state of humiliation compared with the glorious state of the risen Christ; but the day will come when we will lay

aside this mortal body which we now possess and become like Jesus Christ himself.[80]

Our Hearts Must Change First

It is almost impossible to make significant changes in our life by simply willing those changes. It will seem as if every part of our body is trying to resist. Change happens when we turn our lives over to Jesus and allow the transformation process to be completed. We must always realize that there must be a "transformed mind," before there can be a "transformed life!"

Dr. Paul Brand tells the story of Dr. Richard Dawson who learned something about serving in the British Army during World War I. Dawson spent some time in a brutal Japanese prison camp. Daily, he watched soldiers dying of treatable illnesses. Most of the illnesses and infections came from drinking contaminated water in the rivers and swamps near the camp. A little stomach virus, some dehydration–all perfectly treatable during peace time–meant certain death in the prison camp.

One day, Dr. Dawson remembered a piece of advice someone once told him: the water inside of an unripe coconut is almost always sterile. Coconuts grew in abundance around the banks of the swamps. Dr. Dawson began cutting down coconuts and using the water inside as an intravenous fluid for his dehydrated men. Soon, many of the men recovered their health. Dr. Dawson marveled at the fact that those coconuts, full of pure, sterile water, grew beside contaminated swamps and rivers. Evidently, the root system of the tree took in contaminated water–which was killing the men–and turned it into something pure and life-giving.[81]

---

[80] Barclay, 81, 82
[81] Dr. Paul Brand, *God's Forever Feast*, Discovery House Publishers (1993), 90-93

What a beautiful analogy of what Jesus does in our lives. Jesus takes that foul, debilitating part of our life and turns it into something pure and wonderful. He gives us a love and an acceptance we have never known before and makes it possible for us to become all that he has created us to be.

Laying Down our Lives

This transformation process requires that we be willing, as Jesus Christ was, to lay down our lives for our Christian brothers and sisters. We are all familiar with the Scripture that says, *"For God so loved the world that he gave his one and only Son, that whoever believes in him shall not perish but have eternal life"* (John 3:16). But are we also aware of what the apostle John said when he proclaimed: *"This is how we know what love is: Jesus Christ laid down his life for us. And we ought to lay down our lives for our brothers"* (1 John 3:16).

The story is told of a World War I soldier when horror gripped his heart as he saw his lifelong friend fall in battle. Caught in a trench with continuous gunfire whizzing over his head, the soldier asked his lieutenant if he could rescue his friend, "I don't think it will be worth it. Your friend is probably dead and you may throw your own life away." The lieutenant's words didn't matter, and the soldier went anyway.

Miraculously he managed to reach his friend, hoist him onto his shoulder, and bring him back to their company's trench. As the two of them tumbled in together to the bottom of the trench, the officer checked the wounded soldier then looked kindly at his friend. "I told you it wouldn't be worth it," he said. "Your friend is dead, and you are mortally wounded." "It was worth it, though, sir," the soldier said. "How do you mean, 'worth it'" responded the lieutenant? "Your friend is dead!" "Yes sir," the private answered. "But it was worth it because when I got to him, he was still alive, and I had the satisfaction of hearing him say, 'Jim, I knew you'd come.'"[82]

Jesus himself said, *"Greater love has no one than this, that he lay down his life for his friends"* (John 15:13). So you see that to be transformed into the likeness of Jesus requires great sacrifice and commitment. It requires of us that we be selfless instead of selfish. It requires of us that we be willing to give up our lives for the needs of others.

In James Michener's novel *Hawaii*, an old man contracts leprosy. The year is 1870, and lepers are outcasts in Hawaiian society, forced to live in leper colonies far from their loved ones. When the old man shares this sad news with his family, his wife kneels before him and offers herself as his *kokua*. A kokua is a healthy person who willingly commits to staying with and nursing a leprous patient. These kokuas, or "helpers," move to the leper colony and run the risk of catching the disease too. Before they are allowed on the ship that will take them away from their home, an official stands on deck and asks for the final time, "Are you sure you know what you're doing?" One must be committed to be a kokua.

Follow the Pattern

Paul is saying that if you want to be a committed disciple and your citizenship is in heaven, then you must follow my example and take note of those who live according to the pattern we gave you (v. 17). In other words, there is a distinct pattern to living for Christ that can be seen and witnessed in Paul and others who follow his example.

---

[82] Jack Canfield, *This Little Light of Mine*, A Cup of Chicken Soup For The Soul, (1996)

One commentator says of Paul's comments on following a pattern,

> Paul was no egotist here. He had expressed his renunciation of everything for Christ's sake in [chapter 3] verses 7-11, and acknowledged his imperfection in verses 12-14. Indeed, these attitudes are basic to any who would follow Jesus. 'Following' would be recognized by readers, however, as containing all those aspects of Paul's life and teaching which showed forth Christ.[83]

That pattern is seen also of course in the life of Jesus Christ. His life was one of JOY and PEACE in all that He did. He even faced the cross with joy in His heart knowing that the outcome would be a blessing to all who would follow Him (Hebrews 12:2). Paul commanded Timothy and all Christians, *"What you heard from me, keep as the pattern of sound teaching, with faith and love in Christ Jesus"* (2 Timothy 1:13).

It is a fact that Jesus followed the pattern of living as God would have him live. Paul followed the pattern of living as God would have him live. Following the pattern laid down by our Lord is a way of living that is chosen by those who would seek God's will. Sometimes Christians are accused of being like Lemmings.

Someone said that there is one similarity between mice and men. None of us wants to die. Self-preservation is one of the strongest instincts in living creatures. And yet high in the Scandinavian mountains lives a small mouse-like creature

---

[83] Anthony Ash, *The College Press NIV Commentary Philippians, Colossians & Philemon*, College Press, 107

that every few years will commit mass suicide. The creatures are called Lemmings.

They have given us the phrase, "like Lemmings headed for the sea," for that is what they do. Every few years when their population has grown too large and the food supply has become too scarce they leave their burrows and like a mighty army, swarm out of the mountains and rush downward toward the sea. Normally, Lemmings fear and avoid water. During their mass march, however, they brave streams and lakes. They also devour everything in their path.

After running for weeks the Lemmings finally reach the seashore, and then, row upon row, plunge headlong into the water! For a short time the frantic rodents remain afloat, but soon the creatures tire, and one by one sink to their doom.

Many theories have been offered about this mass suicide. Some zoologists argue that the fatal plunge of the Lemmings is just an error in judgment. Perhaps the creatures think the ocean is just one wider river to cross on the way to a larger food supply. All explanations remain only guesses, however. No one really knows what gets into all those suicidal Lemmings.

What would be wrong if we truly were like Lemmings? We are supposed to act in unison in serving our Lord, after all the apostle Paul said,

> *I appeal to you, brothers, in the name of our Lord Jesus Christ, that all of you agree with one another so that there may be no divisions among you and that you may be perfectly united in mind and thought* (1 Corinthians 1:10).

The difference might be in the fact that for us it is a choice. A choice we make because we know of and have experienced the JOY that comes from a complete obedience and submission to His will. Also, because we know the end result will be a transformation of our bodies to be like Christ's glorious body and an abode in heaven with Him forever. Praise the Lord!

Questions for Review

1. How could Jesus face the cross with joy in His heart?
2. What lesson do we learn from the Lemmings?
3. How do you think our bodies will change when Jesus comes?
4. What does "follow the pattern" mean and what pattern?
5. What is the difference between being a "reformer" and being a "transformer?"
6. Why won't new wine exist in old wine skins?
7. Quote 2 Timothy 1:13, and tell what the context is.
8. How can we transform into the likeness of Christ (2 Corinthians 3:18)?

Lesson Eleven
(Chapter 4:1-9)

Joyfully Praising the Lord Always

Therefore, my brothers, you whom I love and long for, my joy and crown, that is how you should stand firm in the Lord, dear Friends!

I plead with Euodia and I plead with Syntyche to agree with each other in the Lord. Yes, and I ask you, loyal yoke fellow, help these women who have contended at my side in the cause of the gospel, along with Clement and the rest of my fellow workers, whose names are in the book of life.

Rejoice in the Lord always. I will say it again: Rejoice! Let your gentleness be evident to all. The Lord is near. Do not be anxious about anything, but in everything by prayer and petition, with thanksgiving, present your requests to God. And the peace of God, which transcends all understanding, will guard your hearts and your minds in Christ Jesus.

Finally, brothers, whatever is true, whatever is noble, whatever is right, whatever is pure, whatever is lovely, whatever is admirable–if anything is excellent or praiseworthy–think about such things. Whatever you have learned or received or heard from me, or seen in me–put it into practice. And the God of peace will be with you.

A lady came to a stop at the red light. She was directly behind a car filled with young children, driven by their mother, and bearing a big bumper sticker: 'Honk–If You Love Jesus.' So the lady in the second car gave a friendly push on the horn, whereupon the mother in the car up front stuck her head out of the window, swore profusely, and yelled, 'Can't you see the light's still red?' Isn't this a little bit like all of us? While we may give 'lip service' to the gospel of Christ as our ethical standard and even use such to severely criticize others around us when they violate plain passages of God's divine word, we personally 'fall short of the glory of God.'[84]

The Worry Complex

If anyone had an excuse for worrying, it was the apostle Paul. What is worry? The Greek word translated "anxious" ('careful' in the KJV) in v. 6 means, *to be pulled in different directions*. Our hopes pull us in one direction; our fears pull us the opposite direction. Worry is the greatest thief of our JOY! The trouble with anxiety is that it can cause us to react to perceived threats in ungodly and sinful ways.

In America today, anxiety and depression are the twin pathologies of daily life. It is estimated that anxiety brings on depression, and that we have over 20 million people suffering with depression (as of this writing) today in America. And over half of them are women. Anxiety is considered a disorder that usually incapacitates an individual. Psychologists state,

---

[84] Terry M. Hightower, *Have You Taught Yourself Lately?* Firm Foundation, November 1992

Anxiety is ubiquitous to the human condition. From the beginning of recorded history, philosophers, religious leaders, scholars, and more recently physicians, as well as social and medical scientists, have attempted to unravel the mysteries of anxiety and to develop interventions that would effectively deal with the pervasive troubling condition of humanity. Today, as never before, calamitous events brought about by natural disasters or callous acts of crime, violence, or terrorism have created a social climate of fear and anxiety in many countries around the world.[85]

When fear keeps on occurring in diverse situations, which are not dangerous, we are probably dealing with neurotic anxiety. Most often, people with neurotic anxiety have little or no idea of what they fear. They just feel the dread hanging over them. They may actually be fearful and worried about such things as rejection or disapproval, physical abuse and harm, criticism, and failure to perform. The fears of other people and what others may say or do are more common than any other causes of anxiety.

Anxious dread may be the signal of guilt and fear of punishment by parents, God, or other power figures. It may also be attributed to shame or fear that other people may form a bad opinion of you. Closely related is embarrassment, the fear that others may make fun of you or mock you. Sometimes the dread appears to be a deep worry that everyone is going to leave and that you will be left helpless and alone. Sometimes it is just jealousy and the desire to have something that somebody else has. The anxiety of such

---

[85] David A. Clark and Aaron T. Beck, *Cognitive Therapy of Anxiety Disorders*, The Guilford Press, 3

feelings can begin to control the heart and purpose of an individual.

Stress Reactions

God created us with built-in mechanisms for responses to a threat. We may not know exactly what caused Euodia and Syntyche to not get along. It seems quite evident that something became a threat to one of them or both of them. Since I believe it is true that "all anger is a response to a perceived threat," I am convinced that the stress they must have experienced produced a threat to their relationship. Sometimes our own greed and ego can cause the stress.

There are physical events our bodies automatically activate under stress. These events, known as the "General Adaptation Syndrome," the "fight or flight response," or the "arousal syndrome," prepare us for coping with danger. The hormone "adrenaline" is responsible for our bodies having extra strength during times of a physical threat. But when we attribute danger to events, which cannot really do us all that much damage, we are liable, by our attributions, to fill up daily life with perceived threats. Then the physical reactions designed for meeting real danger are made to occur frequently or constantly. It can also be true of our perceived threats that are not real but imaginary. When we perceive that we are threatened in terms of our reputation, self-worth, or convictions, we are then prompted to react in angry and hostile ways. Many times our perceived threat is in the area of greed and we seek ways to get our own way.

Malone says in reference to this subject (vs. 6, 7),

> Paul here discloses the secret of the worry-free life. The verse has been translated: *'Worry about nothing, but in every prayer and supplication make your needs known to God thankfully.'* The American Standard

renders it *'In nothing be anxious...'* The word 'anxious' has as its root idea 'the divided mind.' Such a mind is a costly liability and is a certain producer of paralyzing apprehension.

Malone goes on to say,

> Two words are particularly worthy of note: 'nothing' and 'everything.' These are closely related and the latter expression ('in *everything* by prayer and supplication...') shows how the former ('in *nothing* be anxious') is accomplished. If we are to 'worry about *nothing*,' we must pray about *everything* that might be a cause of worry.[86]

Another commentator states,

> Anxiety can produce irritability and defensiveness. It is a soil in which discord could grow. Indeed matters that might otherwise be of lesser moment can reach swollen proportions when fed by anxiety. The verb here rendered 'be anxious' is translated 'take interest' in 2:20. Though anxiety is not specifically addressed elsewhere in the letter, it could clearly be both a cause of and a consequence of the situation in the Philippian church. 'Stop worrying' is the literal meaning, and was more than just a negative commandment. Paul gave a way to stop. As he had often used 'in the Lord' to indicate the special way Christ impacted the Christian life, so here prayer is specified.[87]

---

[86] Malone, 105
[87] Ash, 118, 119

"The Window"

There were once two men, both seriously ill, in the same small room in a great hospital. Quite a small room, just large enough for the pair of them, two beds, two bedside lockers, a door opening onto the hall, and one window looking out on the world. One of the men, as a part of his treatment, was allowed to sit up in bed for one hour in the afternoon, something to do with the draining of fluid from his lungs. And his bed was next to the window. The other man had to spend all of his time flat on his back, and both of them had to be kept quiet and still, which is the reason they were in that small room by themselves. One of the disadvantages was that they weren't allowed to do much, no reading, no radio, no T.V. They would talk hours and hours about their families and their past lives.

Every afternoon when the man was propped up by the window, for his hour, he would pass the time by describing what he would see outside. The other man began to live for that hour. The window apparently overlooked a park where there was a pond, ducks, swans, children playing, young lovers walking hand in hand beneath the trees, and there were flowers, people playing softball, and a fine view of the city skyline. He got to the point where he could enjoy every minute of this, and he could almost see what was happening.

Then one fine afternoon he began to think "why should the other man get to look out the window and not him." He felt ashamed, but in a few days he began to get sour with jealously; he couldn't sleep–he should be by the window and he grew more seriously ill, and the hospital staff couldn't understand it.

One night the man by the window suddenly awoke coughing and choking, his hands groping for the button that would bring the night nurse–but he couldn't reach it; on and on it went until the breathing stopped. The other man continued to stare at the ceiling not willing to reach his button.

After taking the dead man away the next morning, the other man asked if he could be moved to the window. He propped himself laboriously up and looked out the window—he faced a blank wall.[88]

One man reflects the desperate desire for circumstances to make him happy–the other chose the JOY of dreaming and imagining color, beauty, and life to fill the room for both of them. Thus we see the peril of *happiness seeking* over joyfully being thankful for what God has given us.

The Truth About Anger

Many people try to ignore anger or try to make it a sinful emotion that God has condemned. Some people feel that we should never get angry and that if we can rid our life of anger, we will be happy. The problem of anger in our lives cannot be dealt with so simply. Like taxes, anger doesn't just go away, even if we decide it ought to. The truth is that anger is not always bad. God is angry at times (Psalms 7:11; Exodus 4:14; Deuteronomy 29:27). Jesus experienced anger when He saw the hard hearts of the Pharisees and later when He cleansed the Temple (Mark 3:5; John 2:17).

The apostle Paul got angry many times, and one time he got angry with the church at Corinth for not getting angry with the man who was living with his father's wife (1 Corinthians 5). There were other times when the apostle got angry with individuals or churches, but he always had their best interests at heart (Galatians 2:11-14; Acts 16:18; 17:16; 2 Corinthians 7:9-11). We do not see Paul getting angry

---

[88] G. W. Target, *The Window*, Short Drama (1998)

in a vengeful way or with jealousy in his heart. Paul points out the fact that we need to engage in righteous anger, and act accordingly when faced with sin in the church and the world.

The simple emotion of anger is not always harmful or unloving. It is what we do when we are angry that has moral significance. Next to love, anger is the most common emotion experienced in life. Many psychologists believe that anger is the primary emotion experienced by a person in depression.

It is easy in our culture to tell ourselves that we can't control angry feelings. There is a difference between *being* angry and *venting* anger. There is a difference in being *assertive* and being *violent* when expressing anger.

"Venting" is basically a concept, held by some psychiatrists and psychologists, which asserts that our emotions are like a steam boiler, which must release pressure by releasing steam to avoid an explosion. I have never seen any credible research or experimental evidence to confirm this theory. In fact, this theory flies in the face of Scripture. The Bible tells us that we can release our emotions in an acceptable way.

In the book of James, we find a Scripture that encourages us to *"be quick to listen, slow to speak and slow to become angry, for man's anger does not bring about the righteous life that God desires"* (James. 1:19, 20).

A good definition for *righteous anger* would be, "anger under control and for the right reason." In my experience, as a professional counselor, people who have been counseled to use objects or the therapist himself as a target for their venting, have been void of the desire to control their emotions. This process does not encourage self-control. In fact, I believe it does just the opposite. It encourages a lack of self-control.

Whether it is an adult venting or a child throwing a temper tantrum, all venting should be discouraged. In fact, the acceptance of *venting* in our society has caused us to experience a culture where *road rage* is common. Expressing our feelings with control and a caring attitude should be taught as proper behavior.

Anger is defined in most textbooks as, "an emotional response of the mind and body to a stimulus." Paul wrote, *"In your anger do not sin: do not let the sun go down while you are still angry, and do not give the devil a foothold"* (Ephesians 4:26, 27). Paul is telling us, by inspiration from God, to deal with the issue of anger before the day is over. How we deal with our anger is at the heart of the issue of self-control.

Paul makes it plain that we can control our anger, and we had better control it or it will cause us to sin. Anger is an emotional response to a stimulus and when the stimulus is withdrawn, the anger responses will cease. That is, if we don't tell ourselves how unfair and unjust life is.

We need to learn to reject absolute statements and accept the truth, even if it causes us some pain and discomfort. Statements such as, "I can't live without him/her," or "I can't stand it if I'm not liked by everyone," or "It would be terrible if he/she rejected me," should be erased from our minds. Such statements cause a lot of anxiety. Instead, we should tell ourselves truth statements, such as, "I can stand it if I lose a loved one; it will be hard and painful, but I can make it."

The truth is not everyone will like us and it hurts to be rejected by people, but we can deal with it and get on with our lives. When we are rejected we must tell ourselves, "It is not the end of the world!" The Bible teaches us that growth and maturity come from pain and hardship (Hebrews 12:7-11).

Paul is telling us in this section of Philippians that we need not be anxious about anything in this world, but have faith in a God who loves us and wants to give us peace. Most people in the world want peace and never find it because they look in all the wrong places and refuse to believe in the God who has the power to give us peace.

Confusing Attainment with Contentment

Many people think they must have it all. Because we confuse attainment with contentment, we may feel no need for Jesus Christ. Not unless we look deep within our hearts. Dr. Peter Hirsch, author of *Success by Design*, suggests that there is one powerful and profound question which, when asked, reveals our deepest needs and values. And that question is simply, "Are you happy?" He says that the fastest way to get to know someone on a deeper level is to ask them this question, "Are you happy?"; it touches the deepest part of who we are and what we want out of our life.

It was reported that Oprah Winfrey decided to kick off a new season of her television show by giving each of the 276 members of her television audience a new automobile. The audience members at first looked shocked and then they became deliriously happy. They screamed and jumped around. It was a scene of pure bliss. But after the show, they all went home…back to their everyday lives. And I am certain that the happiness they felt on receiving their new automobile soon wore off. Happiness that depends on outward circumstances cannot last because circumstances change.

People may say, "Oh, if I could just change my circumstances, then I would be happy." But rarely does it work. "Oh, if I could just change my spouse, then I would be happy." "Oh, if I could just lose a few pounds…" or "Oh, if I could just retire…."

The list goes on and on. But happiness that Jesus was describing is not dependent on outer circumstances. *"Blessed are the poor in spirit …Blessed are those who mourn…"*

Standing before the grave of a loved one is not the time for jumping up and down screaming with delight. But you can still be blessed, says Jesus (Matthew 5:3-10).

Believing in Jesus Christ is the answer. But accepting Jesus requires more than an emotion or a feeling. Accepting Jesus requires an obedient heart. Jesus said that, *"If you love me you will keep my commandments"* (John 14:15). Receiving Jesus begins with the mind. Do you have a philosophy of life that is satisfying and responsible and in accordance with the Word of God? Some people, when it comes to religion, feel that they must park their brains at the door. And in this post-modern world the word philosophy has come into disfavor. But there are some issues you need to settle in your own mind and heart; having a philosophy of life that has answers to questions that deal with the issues about the universe and God. Issues like the goodness and the steadfastness of God. Even when things are going badly, as things always do from time to time, can you turn them over to God with the assurance that in the end everything will turn out all right? Paul evidently believed that we can be assured that all things work together for good when our faith is in our savior Jesus Christ (Romans 8:28). Such a faith defines THE JOY PRINCIPLE.

Questions for Review

1. What is the author's definition of "anger?"
2. How does the author explain the difference between *attainment* and *contentment*?
3. How does the book of James prove that anger is a choice?
4. How did the story of *The Window* affect you?
5. What is the truth about anger?
6. What does the word *anxious* in the original Greek mean?
7. How would you describe the *fight or flight response*?
8. Is anger a sin? Why or why not?

Lesson Twelve
(Chapter 4:10-13)

Joyfully Learning to Be Content

> *I rejoice greatly in the Lord that at last you have renewed your concern for me. Indeed, you have been concerned, but you had no opportunity to show it. I am not saying this because I am in need, for I have learned to be content whatever the circumstances. I know what it is to be in need, and I know what it is to have plenty. I have learned the secret of being content in any and every situation, whether well fed or hungry, whether living in plenty or in want. I can do everything through him who gives me strength.*

In one of his books, Chuck Swindoll tells about a secret weapon devised by the Russians during the Second World War. Swindoll describes it as the most useless weapon of all time. Swindoll is referring to the so-called "dog mine." The plan was to train dogs to associate food with the undersides of tanks, in hope that they would run hungrily beneath the tanks of the enemy army. Bombs were then strapped to the dog's backs. Unfortunately, the dogs associated food solely with Russian tanks. The plan was begun the first day of Russia's involvement in World War II and abandoned on day two. The dogs with bombs on their backs forced an entire Soviet division to retreat.

When we leave major decisions to man, we see that many times the decisions we make are not wise. Paul said, *"Where is the wise man? Where is the scholar? Where is the philosopher of this age? Has not God made foolish the wisdom of the world"* (1 Corinthians 1:20, 21)?

It is not in man to discover the secret of contentment. Even Jeremiah states: *"I know, O Lord, that a man's life is not his own; it is not for man to direct his steps"* (Jeremiah 10:23).

John MacArthur in his commentary on Philippians states,

> The Greek word translated 'content' in verse 11 appears only here in the New Testament. In extra-biblical Greek it was used to speak of being self-sufficient, having enough, or not being dependent on others. One ancient writer used the word in reference to a country that supplied itself and had no need of imports. True contentment comes only from God, and enables believers to be satisfied and at ease in the midst of any problem.[89]

The Victimization Game

There are counselors and psychologists who believe that the victim mentality in our society hinders those who engage in it, from experiencing contentment. Many people in our world are eager and willing to blame anything and everything but themselves for their behavior. We live in a very litigious society where people are quick to sue anyone for the slightest reasons, and because our courts cater to them, people are not held responsible for their sins (or as some would rather put it, "their mistakes").

We have a great capacity to "shift the blame" in our culture. This propensity goes way back to our original parents. When confronted by God regarding the violation of God's only

---

[89] John MacArthur, *New Testament Commentary*, 299

prohibition in the Garden of Eden, Eve could only say that, "the devil made me do it" (paraphrased). And Adam was no better when he shifted the blame on Eve and God as well (Genesis 3:12, 13). Nothing much has changed since then.

Modern humanistic psychology has been obsessed with the idea that man is not responsible for his conduct. You see it everywhere, on TV and radio talk shows, in the media and in our institutions of higher learning.

In his very insightful book, *Psychological Seduction*, William Kilpatrick states:

> My newfound Bible was psychologist Carl Roger's *On Becoming a Person*. In it Rogers gently suggested that, 'humans are at heart good and decent creatures with no more natural disposition toward hatred than a rosebud. I looked within and found no hate. There were no bad people, I concluded only bad environments.'

Kilpatrick goes on to say,

> Some of the most distinguished psychologists– Coles, Menninger, Bettleheim, Mowrer, Campbell, and Gaylin–have worked in recent years to reinstate concepts of sin and guilt. Others have come to see that self-esteem or the lack of it is too shallow a concept to be of much help in analyzing the human predicament.[90]

It is evident that many, if not all, of the secular counseling theories are based on victimizing the client. They follow the

---

[90] William Kilpatrick, *Psychological Seduction*, Thomas Nelson Publishers, (1983) 17, 86

medical model devised by Sigmund Freud that proclaims all psychological disorders as mental diseases, and therefore, they should be treated as illnesses that are caused by the client's environment. This theory then victimizes and develops a mindset that requires blaming others or the authority figures in one's life as the culprit that caused their illness, rather than accepting blame for their sins or bad choices.

It is believed by some Christian counselors that Freud played a vital part in the present irresponsible interpretation of the psychological human condition as a *medical problem*. From this thinking, a mindset has been widely adhered to in modern times where people believe that the root causes of the pathologies man struggles with in general are evaluated in terms of diseases, rather than the consequences of our sins and wrong choices. Jay Adams, a prominent Christian psychologist, correctly makes the point, "The idea of sickness as the cause of personal problems vitiates all notions of human responsibility."[91]

Perhaps it is too easy to blame Freud for the willingness of our society to play the victim and blame all mishaps and sins on our upbringing. It is one of the main premises of the Bible that man must be ultimately responsible for his behavior. It is evident that this is why biblical counseling, with the mandate of personal responsibility and subjection to the Word of God, is powerful as a therapeutic approach. Counseling is more effective when it comes to helping people face their sins, and applying the remedy found in Scripture.

The apostle Paul refused to be a victim of his circumstances, and determined to be victorious over his environment (a Roman prison) through faith in Jesus Christ.

---

[91] Jay Adams, *Competent to Counsel*, Ministry Resources Library, (1970) 5

The Christian then has a mandate to not be a victim of his emotions or his circumstances, but to put faith in God, because He cares for us, and will deliver us (1 Peter 5:7). Paul said that he would not allow himself to be mastered by anything other than his faith (1 Corinthians 6:12). We are more than conquerors through our faith in and commitment to Jesus Christ (Romans 8:31-39).

Causes of Anxiety

Experts in the field of psychology and psychiatry today tell us that we suffer more from exposure to stress and anxiety in our society than any generation in history. Such assertions are usually accompanied with references to the fast pace of life in our culture. But the idea that stress is purely and simply caused externally is lacking in the facts. Events don't affect us so much as our interpretations and beliefs about them do. Psychological stress is caused, not be events, but by the meaning (interpretation) we attribute to them.

When people go through life believing that certain events would be awful, terrible, dreadful, and catastrophic, the possibility of those things happening creates overwhelming stress. Other people experience the same events, telling themselves that they are merely inconvenient or unpleasant, but survivable. Almost any event to which we assign woeful meaning can be a stressor. Common stressors encountered in counseling others are: separation, divorce, quarrels with others, the death of a spouse, suicide of a loved one, contracting a large debt, losing a job, suffering a physical illness, financial setbacks, and problems with children.

Positive events can be stressful also. Getting married, being promoted, finishing school, getting an advanced degree, increased income, and taking a vacation are examples of events we are commonly involved in that cause stress.

Change may be the major ingredient of stressful events. Change for the worse or for the better. When we attribute threat, horror, or demand to any event involving change, that event becomes stressful. Remember, events of life can be made into stressors. All we have to do is attribute to any of them the traits of a mortal blow and talk to ourselves that way.

Then the physical defense mechanisms designed for meeting real danger are made to occur more frequently. With such constant stress, and the continued release of adrenaline, there is a strong propensity towards this hormone breaking down the body's organs and natural immune systems. The body is not designed for such constant stress. And neither is the mind or the soul.

The Meaning of Contentment

The apostle Paul says in essence that he has *learned* to be content. In other words, it is a learning process. He learned it by trial and error, by experience and faith in his Lord. It is not something that even an inspired apostle has received by revelation from the Lord Jesus Christ. It is not something he experienced by osmosis. The very idea of learning to be content means there was a time when Paul did not have as much contentment as he is experiencing at this point in his life while in a Roman prison.

Malone says,

> Paul's word for 'content' was used commonly by the Stoics to mean 'independent,' 'self-sufficient.' However, here Paul uses it to express a very different kind of sufficiency. Stoicism affirmed that man's true resources were within himself, never in external

Joyfully Learning to Be Content 153

things and circumstances. Paul would agree with the Stoic about external circumstances, but he had a totally different idea about sufficiency. The Stoic asserts, 'I can meet anything in the courage and rectitude of my own soul.' Paul exults, 'I can meet anything and do all things *in him who strengthens me.*' Christ is his sufficiency.[92]

Another commentator states:

The word rendered 'content' is only here in the New Testament [Greek], though cognates are found in 1 Corinthians 9:8 and 1 Timothy 6:6. Philosophers used the word to describe the independence wisdom brought. Paul changed the idea into an independence of dependence on Christ.[93]

Editor Ole Anthony of *The Door* magazine states:

Throughout recorded history, Christians have gloried in their weaknesses, in their humility. It was through these means that they could identify with Christ and his humility and suffering. I worry about a culture in which pastors preach on 'being a winner for Jesus,' and professional athletes claim that Jesus gave them the victory in a game.

Then, Anthony calls to mind a young girl in his congregation named Shannon. Shannon was born with numerous health problems. Shannon will never accomplish great things with her life, as most of us define 'great things.' She will never win any awards or

---

[92] Malone, 113
[93] Ash, 126

academic honors. Few of us would look to Shannon as an example of 'victorious Christian living.'

'But,' Anthony writes, 'she is a thousand times more important to the kingdom of God than all the champions on earth because she's totally without guile or self-seeking. Others learn about love by being around Shannon. They learn about compassion and humility.'[94]

Barclay enlightens us further when he says,

In order to achieve contentment, the Stoics abolished all desires and eliminated all emotions. Love was rooted out of life, and caring was forbidden. As the scholar of ancient history and the New Testament, T. R. Glover, said, 'The Stoics made of the heart a desert, and called it a peace.'

We see at once the difference between the Stoics and Paul. The Stoics said: 'I will learn to be content by a deliberate act of my own will.' Paul said: 'I can do all things through Christ, who infuses his strength into me.' For the Stoics, contentment was a human achievement; for Paul, it was a divine gift. The Stoics were *self-sufficient*; but Paul was *God-sufficient*. Stoicism failed because it was inhuman; Christianity succeeded because it was rooted in the divine. Paul could face anything, because in every situation he had Christ; those who walk with Christ can cope with anything.[95]

---

[94] Ole Anthony, *When did Christians Become Champions?* The Door Magazine, January/February 2005 issue

[95] Barclay, 100

Joyfully Learning to Be Content

The apostle Paul exhorts Christians to not compare ourselves with others (Galatians 6:4). The comparison of the achievement of others diminishes our sufficiency in Christ and demolishes the JOY Principle that should empower our lives. Charles Colson in his wonderful book, *Power Religion*, states:

> Much of the content of conference presentations by evangelical luminaries results in the presenter's impressing the crowd. Pastors in smaller, unadorned churches, with less personal charisma and fewer rhetorical gifts dream, 'If only I were like this person!' Of course, that is not to discount lessons we may learn from their experience, but the fact is, such encouragement as 'Look what I did! And you can do it, too!' is ego-centered and unrealistic. The danger, therefore, is *impersonation* instead of *imitation* [of Jesus Christ].[96]

Unrealistic Expectations

Another JOY stealer in our lives is *unrealistic expectations*. Too often we allow unrealistic expectations to set us up for a fall. They set us up for disappointment and heartbreak. It is not terrible or even unusual if others do things we don't like, or fail to treat us as well as we treat them. We waste a lot of time, energy and thought when we brood over the offenses of others. And if we have expectations of our mate or our children, or anybody in our world, we must evaluate whether or not they are realistic for that person to fulfill.

We do not have the right to be angry when another person does not live up to our expectations. There is no necessary connection between the behavior of another person and our

---

[96] Charles Colson; *Power Religion*, Moody Press, 148-149

anger. It doesn't matter how unfairly, unjustly or thoughtlessly someone has behaved toward us, we are angry because of our own self-talk.

We are all different and many of us come from different backgrounds. To expect everybody in our world to do or be what we want them to be is impossible. Some people may not be able to perform exactly as we expect them to and they may have different belief systems than we have.

All of us have sinned, according to God's Word (Romans 3:23). The people in our lives will not always be kind, just, loving, and thoughtful to us. Learn to deal with it! None of us behave perfectly and fairly in every instance. We must learn to ACCEPT one another, with all of our quirks and idiosyncrasies, just as Christ has accepted us (Romans 15:7).

When we get caught up in the judgment of others, we set ourselves up for frustration and then we lose our Joy. Vindictive anger towards someone, who is unjust and cruel, is usually futile. Such people do not have the same mindset as we do and our judgments are not theirs, and they usually have little effect on the controller or perfectionist in our life. But they do cause us emotional pain and heartache. We can learn to accept people even when we don't condone their behavior. This is the attitude that Paul had towards those who would be his enemies (1:15-18).

In the April 1989 issue of *Cook's Magazine*, Christopher Kimball, publisher and editorial director, unveiled a theory he calls the "Ascending Organ Thesis." "During the '40s, Kimball explains, "you had to have guts."

> People in those days were judged by their courage and drive. The war hero and the self-made man were the models. Then came the '60s, when you had to have heart. People began to value softness, sensitivity, and self-expression. They looked beneath surface

behavior and considered intentions. They sought charisma and sincerity in their leaders.

"The '90s, will belong to the brain. It is called an 'age of cerebral enlightment.' Today the focus is on 'smarts,' the ability to simplify today's complex problems." It is a complex world, and we are constantly reminded of how much we do not know. Well-educated brains are a necessity for such a world. But the most sophisticated brain ever created is inadequate for the really big issues of life. Issues such as life, death, love, fear, hate, and immortality. We can't turn to a computer to deal with such issues.

Albert Einstein once made this interesting observation. "My ideas," said Einstein, "caused people to reexamine Newtonian physics. It is inevitable that my own ideas will be reexamined and supplanted. If they are not, there will have been a gross failure somewhere." Here was one of the most brilliant minds who ever lived and he was saying that his ideas will one day be obsolete. And he was just talking about mathematics. He wasn't even talking about the truly big questions of life.[97]

All is Vanity

Solomon's failure to find bliss was not just a personal one. He failed because of the very lustful nature of life. Solomon discovered the nature of the world. It is a divided world at war with itself. It is a world where order and disorder are in continuous conflict, and there is no sure defense against its evils but through the Lord. The apostle Paul said,

---

[97] Dynamic Preaching, January 2000

Finally, be strong in the Lord and in his mighty power. Put on the full armor of God so that you can take your stand against the devil's schemes. For our struggle is not against flesh and blood, but against the rulers, against the authorities, against the powers of this dark world, and against the spiritual forces of evil in the heavenly realms (Ephesians 6:10-18). Solomon said,

Again I saw vanity under the sun: a person who has no one, either son or brother, yet there is no end to all his toil, and his eyes are never satisfied with riches, so that he never asks, **For whom am I toiling and depriving myself of pleasure?** *This is also vanity, and an unhappy business* (Ecclesiastes 4:7, 8; RSV).

The divine wisdom of both Solomon and Paul tell us that the pursuit of happiness is vanity, futile when it is focused on this world. Christ is the only source of wisdom and the pursuit of true and lasting contentment is found only in Him. Only then will Paul's words become a reality to all who follow His example.

If the apostle Paul can truly say that he was in a process of learning to be content, we can say that no one can achieve such a truth without the ability to do all things through Christ (v. 13). That is why Paul could say he was JOYFULLY finding contentment in Christ Jesus.

Questions for Review

1. What is meant by the term *Victimization Game*?
2. How does being a victim cause us to lose our Joy?
3. What is the meaning of the term, *medical model*, as described in the book?
4. What is the meaning of contentment in the text of 4:11?
5. How would you define *unrealistic expectations* from the book?
6. What did the Stoics believe about contentment?
7. How would you describe the difference between *self-sufficient* and *God-sufficient*?
8. Why don't we have the right to get angry when someone disappoints us?

Lesson Thirteen
(Chapter 4:14-23)

Joyfully Growing in His Grace

Yet it was good of you to share in my troubles. Moreover, as you Philippians know, in the early days of your acquaintance with the gospel, when I set out from Macedonia, not one church shared with me in the matter of giving and receiving, except you only; for even when I was in Thessalonica, you sent me aid again and again when I was in need. Not that I am looking for a gift, but I am looking for what may be credited to your account. I have received full payment and even more; I am amply supplied, now that I have received from Epaphroditus the gifts you sent. They are a fragrant offering, an acceptable sacrifice, pleasing to God. And my God will meet all your needs according to his glorious riches in Christ Jesus.

Greet all the saints in Christ Jesus. The brothers who are with me send greetings. All the saints send you greetings, especially those who belong to Caesar's household.

The grace of the Lord Jesus Christ be with your spirit. Amen.

A man was driving down the road. He passed a traffic camera and saw it flash. Astounded that he had been caught speeding when he was doing the speed limit, the man turned around and, going even slower, passed the camera again. It flashed once more. He couldn't believe it! He turned, going a snail's pace, and passed the camera one more time. Again, he saw the camera flash. He guessed there must be a problem with the camera and went home. Four weeks later he received three traffic fines in the mail–all for not wearing a seatbelt. Life can be cruel!

There is Always Hope

Again Solomon said,

Anyone who is among the living has hope–even a live dog is better off than a dead lion! For the living know that they will die, but the dead know nothing; they have no further reward, and even the memory of them is forgotten. Their love, their hate and their jealousy have long since vanished; never again will they have a part in anything that happens under the sun (Ecclesiastes 9:4-6).

Of course, there is no hope in the afterlife. Our only true hope and destiny are found in our faith and obedience to Christ.

It is good, Solomon said, to partake of life and its activities, remembering that true survival comes from obedience to the Lord. But he also advised accepting one's lot in life and avoiding excessive ambition, for the gains of this life are vanity. Moreover, Solomon found that God knows precisely what He is doing with the world. He has His own lofty reasons for whatever happens, and He has limited our power to comprehend.

Today, we need to heed the advice of the inspired Solomon. In our families we need to emphasize the fact that life is short and to be lived to the fullest. When we say life to the fullest, we don't mean, "to just eat, drink, and be merry." We mean that every family that seeks to be a Christian home must put their priorities in order. Happiness comes, not from the possession of things, or the lusts of the flesh, but the possession of the Spirit of God in our lives (Ephesians 3:14-19).

Solomon also said,

Happy is the man who finds wisdom, and the man who gets understanding, for the gain from it is better than gain from silver and its profit better than gold. She is more precious than jewels, and nothing you desire can compare with her. Long life is in her right hand; in her left hand are riches and honor. Her ways are ways of pleasantness, and all her paths are peace. She is a tree of life to those who lay hold of her; those who hold her fast are called happy (Proverbs 3:13-18; KJV).

Solomon is not emphasizing the wisdom of the world, but the wisdom of the Lord as Solomon views the world.

Guaranteed Satisfaction

I don't know about you, but I have picked up a nasty habit and it's called "eating." Now, eating is one habit you need, we should learn to manage it better, but we need food. Jesus said in His Sermon on the Mount that: *"Blessed are those who hunger and thirst for righteousness, for they will be filled"* (Matthew 5:6). One commentator says of this verse:

Fundamental human needs such as **hunger** and **thirst** are often used in the Old Testament to describe the desperate conditions of those who seek divine intervention. Therefore, those who 'hunger and thirst' are the same group of destitute people who are earlier described as the 'poor' and those who 'grieve.'[98]

We need an appetite. Without it, we are going to die. Food and drink are not luxuries, they are needs. Some years ago survivors of an airplane crash in the Andes Mountains in South America, lived on their dead comrades. The gnawing pains of hunger led them to an act that is repulsive to civilized society.

The fact is that very few of us in modern conditions of life know what it is to be really hungry or thirsty. In the ancient world it was very different. It was the hunger of the man who is starving for food, and the man who will die unless he drinks that Jesus is talking about.

How much do you want goodness in your life? How much do you want to be righteous? Do you want it as much as a starving man wants food? The man who is blessed materially is not necessarily the man who seeks to achieve goodness, but the man who longs for it with his whole heart will seek it above all else.

What is righteousness? It means keeping the commandments of God (John 14:15). It does not mean sinlessness (1 John 1:7-9). It is a way of life (Galatians 2:20). Have you ever known a child who lives life with gusto? If he becomes quiet and listless all of a sudden and doesn't want to eat, do you wonder why? A loss of appetite is one of the first symptoms of diminishing health.

---

[98] Chouinard, 97

There is a disorder that is well-known in our society called **anorexia nervosa**; it is a loss of the hunger drive or appetite. In the 1980's a famous group called the Carpenters, with a lead singer Karen Carpenter, made the headlines when it was revealed that she was suffering with anorexia nervosa. Then in 1983, at age 32, she died having starved herself to death. It was a shocker and a surprise that such a wonderfully talented singer would die such a death. She literally starved herself through fear of becoming fat to the point that she no longer had an appetite. The doctors did all they could to save her but to no avail.

The Hebrew writer addresses the subject of the spiritual appetite. He states:

It is impossible for those who have once been enlightened, who have tasted the heavenly gift, who have shared in the Holy Spirit, who have tasted the goodness of the word of God and the power of the coming age, if they fall away, to be brought back to repentance, because to their loss they are crucifying the Son of God all over again and subjecting him to public disgrace (Hebrews 6:4-6).

When a Christian has lost the appetite for spiritual blessings in this life, it is impossible to regain the taste of spiritual food again. It is not that God will not forgive them if they come back to Him. It is a psychological process of rejecting the life God has provided us in this world, with the power of prayer, the promise of eternal life, the blessings of the Word of God, and the joy of the church fellowship etc., and the result is spiritual anorexia nervosa. People can lose their appetites spiritually under certain conditions, such as:

Unconfessed sin. When you are living in unconfessed sin you have no craving after righteousness (Hebrews 10:26).
Self-satisfaction. Self-satisfaction insulates us from an appetite for the things of God (Revelation 3:14-18).
Misunderstanding. What triggers our appetites most: "Leftover hash" or "steak and potatoes"? Some people have no hunger for righteousness because it doesn't seem to be very satisfying. Some people see *righteousness* as "Phariseeism" or as a "loss of individuality."

A hearty appetite is a promise of health. Jesus said, *"For they shall be satisfied."* God fills us up completely, progressively, and permanently (John 10:10). Thank God you can't overeat spiritually. Part of our difficulty is that we have a tendency to hunger and thirst after **happiness** or hunger and thirst after **experience**; and we never seem to receive permanent joy from either one!

God will meet all Our Needs

Jackson writes,

> Finally, Paul writes: *'And my God shall supply every need of yours according to his riches in glory.'* Notice, that just as the Philippians had fully supplied the needs of Paul, so God would fully supply theirs. This is a perfect illustration of the principle of 'sowing and reaping' (Galatians 6:7). In Christ, God will fully supply all our needs to serve Him, which is the purpose of our existence.
>
> This promise of God's care would certainly be meaningful to the brethren in Philippi. One remembers, for example, that Paul had earlier noted the woefully impoverished conditions in Macedonia.

When a contribution was being collected for the poor among the saints in Judea (1 Corinthians 16:1-2; Romans 15:26), the Macedonians had given out of their 'deep poverty.' So pitiful was their condition that Paul was inclined not to accept their gift. They, however, begged him with much entreaty (2 Corinthians 8:1-4). What a magnificent group of saints![99]

The apostle Paul is *joyfully growing in God's grace* even though he is an apostle and in a Roman prison. He has experienced the learning process of being content in all circumstances. He revels in the dependency he has in God's power and mercy. He prays that the Philippian Christians, and all disciples in Christ, will experience such contentment as well.
Malone proclaims,

> The Philippians have endeavored to meet Paul's immediate material needs; now the apostle, in turn assures them that God will care for their needs: 'And my God shall supply every need of yours according to his riches in glory in Christ Jesus' (4:19). The Christian's provision: '*Every* need of yours' God will supply! From the cradle to the grave man is bombarded by an incessant, insistent sense of need. Even temporal needs will be supplied (Matthew 6:24-33). But going far beyond that, the great heart hungers–the need for pardon, for peace, for spiritual power–God satisfies according 'to his riches in glory in Christ Jesus.'[100]

The greatest need of all is to know that we have eternal

---

[99] Jackson, 160
[100] Malone, 122

life and that our destiny does not end at death, but that death for the Christian launches a new life with Christ. In Philip Yancey's book, *I Was Just Wondering*, he tries to imagine a society in which no one believed in an afterlife. What would the world look like if no one believed that there was a heaven or a hell? Yancey gave his fictitious land the name of Acirema. These are just a few of the characteristics his imaginary Aciremens would have:

> Aciremans would put great emphasis on youth. The idea of growing old and eventually dying would be so traumatic that they could have no hope for the future. Therefore, preserving their youth would become an obsession. Old age, and anything associated with aging, would be shunned and devalued. In this way, the rest of society could continue the charade of denying the facts of aging. Every kind of cosmetic and chemical treatment that can possibly slow down the aging process would be necessary.
>
> Appearances would be all that matter. Inner beauty, characterized by such things as integrity, compassion, and decorum, would no longer matter. People who do not look attractive, young, and healthy would face great discrimination. Scientists would try to figure out how to eliminate death. People would use all kinds of euphemisms to say that someone has died. Religion for the Aciremans would consist of philosophies to help them make the most of here and now. Eternal rewards wouldn't exist in their belief system, so Aciremen religion would teach that one must be fully gratified and rewarded in this lifetime. Therefore, Aciremans would be taught to 'grab all the gusto they can get,' to build up riches and satisfy their whims and desires as soon as they can.

Does this sound familiar with the status of how our current American culture is operating. The fact is that the word Acirema spelled backward is America.

Another commentator states:

> The outburst of doxology prolongs the theme of God's *glory* which is ascribed to him who is *our God and Father*. The thought now is one of praise rendered to God in acknowledgment of thankfulness for all his goodness and grace. It expresses, too, Paul's own gratitude for the response of God's people to his need, and the intimate fellowship with them in his gospel ministry. 'The doxology flows from the joy of the whole Epistle,' says Bengel, i.e., it is Paul's fitting response to all the things which cause him joy in his prison experience. The liturgical *Amen*, lit. 'confirmed,' derived from a Hebrew verb 'to be firm,' underlies the truth of the doxology, as the writer and reader associate themselves with the confession and own it as valid and true for themselves.[101]

The Purpose of the Heart

The apostle Paul is closing out this letter to the Philippians with a salutation of thankfulness and grace. He sees in the Philippian church a sense of purpose of the heart. Not only did they give abundantly to the needed saints in Judea, but they gave beyond their means. In other words, they were in poverty themselves. Their hearts were judged by Paul as having a noble purpose, and therefore they were commended as having a heart for God.

Author Tommy Barnett tells a revealing story of an encounter with rock-and-roll icon Elvis Presley many years ago.

---

[101] Martin, 189

Elvis was in the congregation at a church where Barnett was speaking. Elvis seemed moved by the sermon, and wanted to talk to Barnett afterwards. Elvis grew up a deeply religious young man. He cut his teeth singing Gospel music. He knew that he needed to repent of his current lifestyle and return to his Christian faith. But the allure of show business was too strong. With tears rolling down his face, Elvis asked, '...what if I renounce show business and find that serving God won't bring joy to my heart?'[102]

That is an honest question many people might ask: What if I renounce this illicit relationship and find that serving God won't bring joy to my heart? What if I give up this destructive habit and find that serving God won't bring joy to my heart? What if I let go of my poisonous attitudes and find that serving God won't bring joy to my heart? Of course, we all know what show business did to the king of rock-and-roll. It did what it has done to so many other talented young stars.

At a crossroads moment, Elvis Presley chose to follow his own desires. Eventually, those desires devoured his very life. The problem is that God gave us a purpose of the heart, and that purpose was not to use the world and all its pleasures and power to find happiness, but to have a personal relationship with Jesus Christ and experience the JOY that is beyond happiness. It is the heart that pursues TRUTH over HAPPINESS and knows the difference. It is the purpose of the heart of the true disciple of Christ to understand what the Lord felt in his heart when he was about to face the Cross: *"...who for the JOY set before Him endured the cross, scorning its shame, and sat down at the right hand of the throne of God"* (Hebrews 12:2).

This belief system is the heart of THE JOY PRINCIPLE!

---

[102] Tommy Barnett, *Adventure Yourself*, Creation House, 126

Questions for Review

1. What is the purpose that God has for our hearts?
2. How would you define *righteousness*?
3. What does it mean to have a spiritual *appetite*?
4. When is happiness a wholesome pursuit?
5. How would you rate the book of Philippians in terms of favorite?
6. Why was Paul so pleased with the Philippian church?
7. How would you define the *purpose of the heart*?
8. How long does God allow us to reject His blessings?

Bibliography

Adams, Jay E.; *Competent to Counsel*, Zondervan Publishing House, 1970

Adams, J. McKee; *Biblical Background*, Broadman Press, 1965

Ash, Anthony L.; *The College Press NIV Commentary on Philippians, Colossians, Philemon*, College Press Publishing Company, 1994

Bales, James D.; *The Law in the Heart*, Gospel Teachers Publications, 1981

Backus, William; & Chapian, Marie; *Telling Yourself The Truth*, Bethany House, 1985

Barclay, William; *The Mind of St. Paul*, Harper & Row Publishers, 1958

Barclay, William; *The Letters to the Philippians, Colossians, and Thessalonians*, The New Daily Study Bible, Westminster John Knox Press, 1975

Barnes, Albert; *Notes on the New Testament–Ephesians, Philippians and Colossians*, Baker Book House, 1965

Beck, Aaron T. & Clark, David A.; *Cognitive Therapy of Anxiety Disorders*, The Guilford Press, 2010

Brand, Paul & Yancey, Philip; *Fearfully and Wonderfully Made*, Zondervan Publishing House, 1980

Bruce, Alexander Balmain, *St. Paul's Conceptions of Christianity*, T & T Publishers, 1896

Bullinger, Ethelbert, W.; *A Critical Lexicon and Concordance to the English and Greek New Testament*, Zondervan Publishing House, 1975

Cloud, Henry & Townsend, John; *Boundaries in Marriage*, Zondervan Publishers, 1999

Colson, Charles, Packer, J.I., Sproul, R.C., McGrath, Alister; *Power Religion*, Moody Press, 1992

Davis, John, D.; *Davis Dictionary of the Bible*, Royal Publishers, 1973

Durant, Will; *Caesar and Christ*, Simon and Schuster, 1944

Fitch, Alger; *Philippians*, Alger Fitch Publishing, 2001

Gardner, Lynn; *Where is God When We Suffer?* College Press, 2007

Gay, Peter; *The Freud Reader*, W. W. Norton & Co., 1989

Gilliam, Doyle; *The Epistle to the Philippians*, Sunset Institute Press, 2009

Ham, Ken; *The Lie–Evolution*, Master Books, 1987

Hamilton, W. T.; *Show Us The Father*, Nichols Brothers Publishing Co. 1964

Hassan, Steven; *Combatting Cult Mind Control*, Park Street Press, 1988

Healy, Jane M.; *Endangered Minds*, Simon & Schuster, 1990

Jackson, Wayne; *Rejoice With Me*, Courier Publications, 2007

Jackson, Wayne; *Acts-From Jerusalem To Rome*, Courier Publications, 2000

Jackson, Wayne; *Before I Die–Paul's Letters to Timothy and Titus*, Courier Publications, 2007

Kilpatrick, William; *Psychological Seduction*, Thomas Nelson Publishers, 1983

MacArthur, John; *New Testament Commentary-Philippians*, Moody Press, 2001

McDowell, Josh; *The Resurrection Factor*, Here's Life Publishers, 1981

Malone, Avon; *Press to the Prize*, 21st Century Christian, 1991

Martin, Ralph P.; *Philippians*, The Tyndale New Testament Commentaries, William B. Eerdmans Publishing Company, 1987

McGuiggan, Jim; *Jesus–Hero of Th*y Soul, Howard Publishing Co., 1998

Robertson, A. T.; *Word Pictures in the New Testament*, Volume IV, The Epistles of Paul, Baker Book House, 1931

Packer, J.I., Tenney, Merril C., White, William, Jr.; *Daily Life in Bible Times*, Thomas Nelson Publishers, 1982

Sanders, Phil; *Let all the Earth Keep Silence*, Star Bible Publications, 1989

Sanders, Phil; *A Faith Built on Sand*, Gospel Advocate Co., 2011

Shelley, Rubel; *In Step With The Spirit–A Study of the Fruit of the Spirit*, 20th Century Christian, 1987

Smith, LaGard F.; *The Cultural Church*, 20th Century Christian, 1992

Smith, LaGard F.; *When Choice Becomes God*, Harvest House Publishers, 1990

South, Tommy; *That We May Share His Holiness*, Bible Guides, 1997

Swindoll, Charles, R.; *The Man of Grace and Grit - Paul*, Thomas Nelson Publishers, 2002

Swindoll, Charles, R.; *Hand Me Another Brick*, Thomas Nelson Publishers, 1978

Thayer, Joseph Henry; *Greek-English Lexicon of the New Testament*, Baker Book House, 1977

Vine, W. E., *Vine's Expository Dictionary of New Testament Words*, MacDonald Publishing Company

White, John: *Eros Defiled–The Christian & Sexual Sin*, Inter-Varsity Press, 1977

Wilson, Ken; *Faith That Makes A Difference*, Agape Publishing, 2010

Wilson, Ken; *The Transformed Life*, Agape Publishing, 2009

CPSIA information can be obtained at www.ICGtesting.com
Printed in the USA
BVOW11s1606150114

341777BV00008B/124/P